WHAT TO DO
WHEN WHAT YOU DID
Didn't Work

THE THERAPIST'S HANDBOOK TO
Overcome Resistance and Achieve
Great Results with Challenging Clients

LEONIE & JOHN O'CONNELL
The Academy of **Therapeutic Hypnosis**

Mind Potential Publishing
by *The Potentialist*

Copyright © 2021 Leonie and John O'Connell and the Academy of Therapeutic Hypnosis.

ALL RIGHTS RESERVED. No part of this book may be reproduced or transmitted in any form whatsoever, electronic, or mechanical, including photocopying, recording, or by any informational storage or retrieval system without the expressed written permission from the author and publisher.

Authors: Leonie and John O'Connell
Title: What to Do When What You Did Didn't Work
ISBN Paperback: 978-1-922380-12-8
ISBN Kindle: 978-1-922380-14-2

 A catalogue record for this book is available from the National Library of Australia

Category: Psychology | Self Help Techniques

Publisher: Mind Potential Publishing
A division of Mind Design Centre Pty Ltd,
PO Box 6094, Maroochydore BC, QLD, Australia.

Publisher Australia: 1300 664 544 www.mindpotentialpublishing.com
Publisher International: +61 405 138 567

Academy of Therapeutic Hypnosis: www.aoth.com.au
Academy of Therapeutic Hypnosis International +61 405 682 647

Cover design by: NGirl Design | www.ngirldesign.com.au

LIMITS OF LIABILITY | DISCLAIMER OF WARRANTY:

The authors and publisher of this book have used their best efforts in preparing this material and they disclaim any warranties, (expressed or implied) for any particular purpose. The information presented in this publication is compiled from sources believed to be accurate at the time of printing, however the publisher assumes no responsibility for omissions or errors. The authors and publisher shall not be held liable for any loss or other damages, including, but not limited to incidental, consequential, or any other. This publication is not intended to replace or substitute medical or professional advice, the authors and publisher disclaim any liability, loss or risk incurred as a direct or indirect consequence of the use of any content.

Mind Potential Publishing bears no responsibility for the accuracy of the information provided as either online or offline links contained in this publication. The use of links to websites does not constitute an endorsement by the publisher. The publisher assumes no liability for content or opinion expressed by the authors. Opinions expressed by the Authors do not represent the opinion of Mind Potential Publishing or Mind Design Centre Pty Ltd.

Printed in Australia

WHAT TO DO
WHEN WHAT YOU DID
Didn't Work

THE THERAPIST'S HANDBOOK TO
Overcome Resistance and Achieve
Great Results with Challenging Clients

LEONIE & JOHN O'CONNELL
The Academy of **Therapeutic Hypnosis**

WHY NOT HAVE LEONIE AND JOHN O'CONNELL AS A GUEST ON YOUR PODCAST, OR AT YOUR NEXT CONFERENCE, FESTIVAL OR EVENT?

ACADEMY OF THERAPEUTIC HYPNOSIS www.aoth.com.au

Tel: Aust: 1300 788 909 | **International:** +61 405 682 647
Email: info@aoth.com.au | **Website:** www.aoth.com.au

Leonie and John O'Connell are the co-founders and Directors of The Academy of Therapeutic Hypnosis. They bring a passion for excellence to the therapeutic field and teach their internationally accredited Fastrack Hypnotherapy Certifications. It is comforting for a newly qualified Practitioner to know that they are supported by their instructor with 12 months mentoring following graduation. This ensures consistent and replicable results for the graduate and their business. The Academy has graduates all over Australia who have purposeful and financially rewarding careers helping others.

BOOKS BY LEONIE AND JOHN O'CONNELL

WHAT TO DO WHEN WHAT YOU DID DIDN'T WORK
The Therapist's Handbook to Overcome Resistance and Achieve Great Results with Challenging Clients.

For Therapists, Clinical Hypnotherapists, Counselors, Psychologists, NLPers and Life Coaches. This book reveals the difference between an ineffective therapy or coaching program and a truly dynamic one. Brimming with often overlooked steps to transform a good therapist or coach into an exceptional one, ensuring that what you do works every time.

ONLINE PROGRAM BY LEONIE AND JOHN O'CONNELL
The Practitioner Masterclass – Overcome Resistance with Challenging Clients

An online qualification brought to you by The Academy of Therapeutic Hypnosis.

ACADEMY QUALIFICATION TRAINING

Qualifying with The Academy of Therapeutic Hypnosis includes 12 months mentoring to ensure confidence in your new skillset and ongoing business success. This means that training courses fill quickly. The AOTH is renowned worldwide for its quality of content and support for graduates after graduation. For the next available Clinical Hypnotherapy Certification and Fastrack training dates refer to the website www.aoth.com.au

Academy of Therapeutic Hypnosis
www.aoth.com.au

Download free book resources from the authors
www.therapistshandbook.com/resources

DEDICATION

This book is dedicated to our past graduates who achieve outstanding results in the world of therapy and improve this planet – one life at a time.

To our future students who have yet to make their impact on this world, and to all of our clients who inspire us to be the best therapists possible.

We also dedicate this book to our children and grandchildren who are our inspiration for everything we do and everything we are yet to achieve.

CONTENTS PAGE

Introduction		9
Chapter 1:	The Essentials of Great Pretalk to Break Through Client Resistance	19
Chapter 2:	The 5 Keys to Set Your Client up for Success	37
Chapter 3:	Great Expectations – Whose Are They Anyway?	53
Chapter 4:	What to Do When the Client Says, "It didn't work."	65
Chapter 5:	Identify and Eliminate Secondary and Tertiary Gains	75
Chapter 6:	What Next – When You Think You've Done Absolutely Everything?	87
Chapter 7:	Pull Out the Big Guns – Expert Tips from Global Leaders	109
Chapter 8:	How to Expand your Practice to Work Online	131
What Your Future Holds		141
Appendix:	The Structure of a Great Pretalk	146
Bonus Content:	How to Set Up a Successful Clinic	150
Meet the Contributors		161
References and Recommended Reading		165
Meet the Authors		167
What Others Have to Say		168

INTRODUCTION

"The distance between where your client is now and where they desire to be, is only separated by what you do."
John O'Connell

The fact that you are in possession of this book suggests that you are searching for answers. Sometimes, as therapists, whether your therapy is psychology, hypnotherapy, counseling, life coaching or another modality, you feel a bit overwhelmed and frustrated when what you do with one client works, but when you use the same process with another client, it simply doesn't work – or at least not as well as you hoped or expected.

This doesn't mean you have failed; it simply means that the information you have and the techniques you are currently using have not succeeded with this particular client and this specific challenge.

You simply need more information and perhaps a different approach, or perspective, however, finding the information you need is not always easy.

What you will learn from the following pages aims to help you resolve the challenges that take up your headspace after treating a client and those niggling thoughts that sometimes keep you awake at night.

> This book will take you through our tried and tested processes that break through the difficulties encountered by therapists when they come across clients who seem resistant or particularly challenging.

INTRODUCTION

What I found after completing my initial training many years ago, was that I had a grasp of the fundamentals I needed, but it wasn't enough. I was missing the keys to make my business a success and achieve great results with every client, every time. My enthusiasm was high, but my confidence was low as I struggled to find techniques, scripts and strategies that I hoped would work for each client. I had a good basic grounding in the application of therapeutic principals. I understood how things should work, but I was left perplexed when the results I was getting were not always as successful as I had hoped.

I became hungry for better results for my clients and a wider breadth of skills and techniques to confidently draw upon. In the years since, my thirst for knowledge grew, I have studied with many world-renowned teachers such as Michael Yapko, Bryan Perry, Tad James, Melissa Tiers and many others. I've been trained in the application of many different techniques and modalities. My results began to soar, my confidence blossomed, and my therapy business reached amazing heights. I began receiving requests from other therapists to mentor them to achieve similar results. I have now trained and mentored a variety of other therapists from modalities such as psychology, counseling, trauma therapy and life coaching.

What I have come to realize is that, at some stage in our therapy careers, we all come across similar issues. Sometimes the therapy is amazing, sometimes it is helpful and yet sometimes there seems to be little or no marked improvement at all and it leaves you baffled as to why. When that happens a variety of thoughts go through your mind:

- ☐ The techniques I used worked on someone else, why not this client?
- ☐ What did I do wrong?
- ☐ What could I have done differently?

For me, these kinds of questions started very soon after my initial training and motivated me to go on a path of discovery to learn why some clients easily achieve results that could seemingly be described as magical, while others are left disillusioned and disappointed. And why both sets of results can be achieved by the same therapist working with similar issues and techniques, yet with different clients.

I wanted answers as to why some therapists get consistently great results, while others get mediocre or poor results, again, using the same therapy models.

So, what is happening here?

- ☐ Is it the therapist?
- ☐ Is it the therapy?
- ☐ Is it the client?
- ☐ Is it a combination of all three?
- ☐ Or is it simply a phenomenon that can't logically be explained? And is logic even at play here?

Logic or Magic?

Many astounding results that my hypnotherapy clients have achieved in the past just don't seem to be logical. The part of the mind we are working with during a hypnotherapy session (or any other process that influences the unconscious part of the mind to elicit positive change) does not work with logic or rationality.

As therapists, we've witnessed it many times, there is no logic or rationale to explain addictive patterns that lead to the use of dangerous substances or the fact that someone continues to smoke cigarettes despite the fact that they desperately don't want to and know all the dangerous health risks.

There seems to be no logic or rationale to the reality that despite the fact that someone desperately wants to be slim, feel great and wear clothes that look fabulous, they eat far too much food for their bodies and force themselves to store excess fat. They know 'what to do' but continue to damage their health and destroy their self-image.

INTRODUCTION

There is really no logic or rationale to the fact that people move from one abusive relationship to another when all they want is to feel safe and loved ... or that others suffer anxiety and panic attacks despite the fact that they are safe and secure in their life. It is difficult to rationalize why someone feels depressed to the point of suicide despite the fact that they have so many reasons to feel good about life.

We can try to analyze and intellectualize these patterns, but the simple truth is that no matter how much we consciously examine these occurrences, they arise from a deeper, 'feeling' level of the mind that isn't motivated by, or listening to, rational or logical reasoning.

I have treated a great many clients, as I'm sure you have too, who say things like, *"I have a great life, a good family, a successful career, and yet I feel so anxious and depressed. I have every reason to feel good, but I don't. I just can't understand why I feel this way."*

So, when we work with these issues, we are certainly not working with the rational part of the mind. If we were, our clients would easily resolve their issues with logic.

Psoriasis

It would be difficult to rationalize why one of my clients, a beautiful young woman from India, had suddenly developed psoriasis all over her body. The condition was totally non-responsive to medical treatment and yet, after just three hypnotherapy sessions the psoriasis totally disappeared. In those sessions we delved into the deeper recesses of the unconscious mind and uncovered and resolved the underlying emotional cause of the condition.

Paralysis

It would be difficult to rationalize why another client, a 65-year-old man with no medical explanation for paralysis that meant he couldn't walk, walked again after just three hypnotherapy sessions that delved deep into the unconscious mind to resolve the challenge.

I have often had clients comment that they have had different types of therapy or life coaching in the past and it worked amazingly well for them. I have also had clients tell me that the treatment they had sought in the past hadn't worked at all. I guarantee at some point, any therapist who sees a large number of clients will have this same experience.

Why Didn't It Work?

Many clients I see tell me they have done months, or even years of counseling or psychology sessions with little or no improvement, yet others find it valuable. Many have had hypnotherapy before with little or no improvement, yet others find it amazingly beneficial.

What is the common denominator?

I started asking questions in an attempt to find a common thread.

- ☐ Why does a treatment work?
- ☐ Why doesn't a treatment work?
- ☐ What could I do differently to ensure **consistently great outcomes** for all of my clients **all of the time?**

INTRODUCTION

An interesting observation I've made on this journey is that many therapists don't really know for sure what type of outcomes their clients have achieved because they don't follow up and ask the question.

Many therapists metaphorically 'cross their fingers' and hope for the best. Or they consider 'no feedback' as 'positive feedback'. Perhaps deep in their unconscious, they are afraid of a negative response, so they avoid seeking feedback at all?

After interviewing many therapists, especially those in the early years after their initial training where there had been no support or mentoring after their course finished, I learned that this was often the case.

Many therapists metaphorically 'cross their fingers' and hope for the best. Or they consider 'no feedback' as 'positive feedback'.

Throughout this book you will realize that many therapists have these same insecurities and you are not alone in the 'hope for the best' and 'avoid confirming it' self-talk.

The danger is that we could be missing important opportunities to learn and grow if we avoid the opportunity to listen and improve. AND, a biggie, is that we miss the opportunity to develop a loyal and successful client base by neglecting to contact them to resolve any challenges they may be experiencing.

Being a hypnotherapist, life coach, psychologist or counselor can feel like an isolated profession. Often, even if we seek guidance from others in the same field, we cannot find the specific answers we search for. The people we seek guidance from often don't have the answers when the questions become challenging. Or we are seen as a competitor and information can be sparse or withheld.

Sometimes we just don't know where to look. Or the information we are given, for some reason, still doesn't work for our client's specific challenge.

In this book I share all that I have learnt with regard to the challenges we face when clients do not seem to achieve the outcome they have come to you for. There are many reasons why what you did with one client yesterday worked and why it's not working with today's client. My purpose is to help you work through the potential reasons and provide opportunities and techniques to improve your results.

All solutions and strategies provided in this book have been tried and tested with great results in real life practice.

I will share strategies and solutions for overcoming resistance and achieving great results with challenging clients; solutions that I have learnt from my own mentors and colleagues and those that I have personally developed or adapted to achieve better outcomes. I'll also share the top tips from my colleagues from around the world who are global leaders in their field. I personally believe it's important to gather all the wisdom we can which is already available to us from this industry, to interpret that wisdom in our own way and become our own unique therapist.

The answers and solutions in this book may not always be what you expect or even agree with. The strategies may seem to be a bit 'out there' for some. All solutions and strategies provided in this book have been tried and tested with great results in real life practice. The approach may seem a bit 'out of the box' so to speak, but to me and to my students, it's not necessarily the technique that matters. The only thing that really matters for the client or the therapist is achieving great results through a client-centered approach. And that means, if what you know so far hasn't worked, then it's time to try something a bit different.

INTRODUCTION

When you have a fresh perspective, you discover new approaches to old issues which will enhance the way you practice and work with clients. So, let's get started!

To your continued success,

Leonie and John

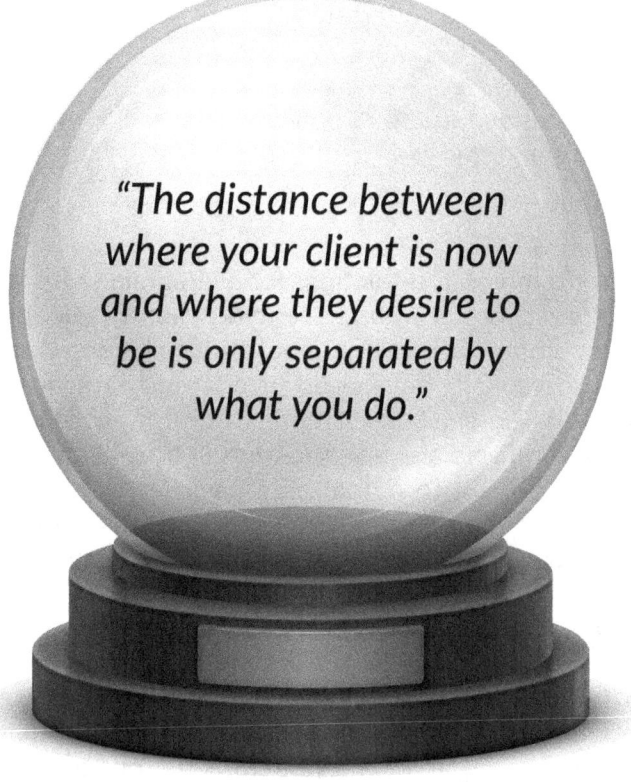

"The distance between where your client is now and where they desire to be is only separated by what you do."

THE ROAD TO SUCCESS STARTS WITH A GREAT PRE-TALK

CHAPTER 1

The Essentials of Great Pretalk to Break Through Client Resistance

> *"Sometimes we create our own failures through the picture in our head of how it's supposed to be."* John O'Connell

Why is an effective pretalk imperative to the success of your sessions?

One of the gems I took away from the first course in hypnotherapy that I ever attended, was the importance of a great pretalk. Even though the course itself was mediocre at best, I am grateful that I learned that gem early in my career. Since then, the importance of the pretalk has been reinforced to me both in my work with clients, and also in my training of students. What we focus on in our first minutes together with our client, correlates directly to their successful outcomes.

The Pocket Watch

When I first started my clinical practice, I operated out of a busy medical center. One Saturday afternoon at closing time, I was standing on the verandah waiting for the rain to ease so I could run out to my car. Another woman was doing the same thing and she struck up a conversation.

> *What we focus on in our first minutes together with our client, correlates directly to their successful outcomes.*

"Are you new to this practice?" she asked. "I haven't noticed you here before."

"Yes" I replied. "I'm a hypnotherapist."

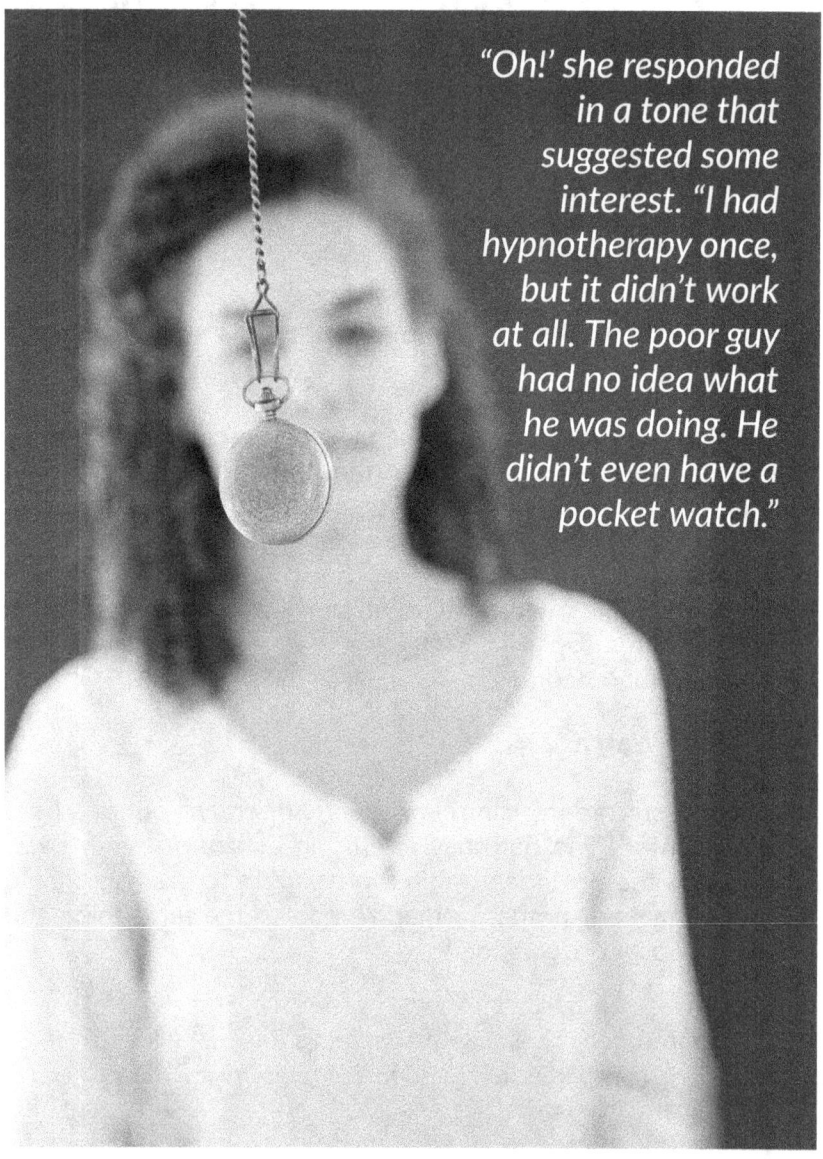

"Oh!' she responded in a tone that suggested some interest. "I had hypnotherapy once, but it didn't work at all. The poor guy had no idea what he was doing. He didn't even have a pocket watch."

At the time, this was a totally bizarre comment to me. We are often taught in our clinical training to protect the industry from these kinds of 'myths', and yet … this woman's false assumptions and expectations were exactly why she believed hypnosis did not work. She actually expected the hypnotherapist to wave a watch in front of her eyes. This is a true story!

Acknowledge the Client's B.S. (Belief Systems)

This instantly signaled to me how misinformed some people are and how the 'B.S.' (belief systems) regarding the 'Hollywood' versions of hypnosis and a hypnotist are still the reality for many people outside of the industry.

I realized back then, that right from the outset, the therapist must align the client's expectations with the reality of what they are about to experience. The 'B.S.' (belief systems) that the client brings into the session will definitely impact the outcome of the therapy. If they expect a particular experience, but then what they actually experience is something else entirely, it consciously and unconsciously leaves the client feeling 'cheated.'

This may leave them with resistance to their session because they believe 'the therapist didn't have a clue about what they were doing'. Frustratingly, the therapy doesn't achieve the desired results and the therapist is oblivious to what went wrong. They never hear from the client again and the B.S. continues to interfere with the client's results until either:

  A. A therapist with skills actually uses a watch

  B. A therapist with skills addresses the B.S. and re-educates the client's expectations.

The same dynamic occurs in all modalities. I have had client's express frustration to me that their psychology sessions were little more than an expensive 'chat session'. Or their counseling sessions were unproductive because the counselor didn't really provide any solutions.

Had the client understood that the psychologist was leading the conversation in a particular direction for a very specific reason … or had the psychologist realized that the client felt little or no benefit from their 'chats', the therapy may have taken quite a different pathway and the outcome may have been much more successful.

Likewise, had the client realized that the counselor was not looking to provide solutions, but was assisting the client to discover their own resources … or had the counselor realized that the client was misinterpreting the counselors intentions and expected something very different from the process, the therapy may have taken quite a different pathway and the outcome may have been much more successful.

Assess the Therapist's 'B.S.' (Belief Systems)

It's important to appreciate that, just as the client's expectations may differ from the reality of the situation, the therapist's 'B.S' might also lead them to make assumptions about the client's knowledge, goals and expectations that are also simply not correct.

John's story

Early in my career, John came to me with anxiety and depression issues. To me, he seemed to be the sort of person who was open minded and very imaginative. One of the processes that I used with him was Time Line Therapy. I made the assumption that he would be the type of client who would respond well to this. My assumption was correct and the result was nothing short of astounding. He regressed to a particular event from when he was two weeks old and the impact it had on his treatment and his wellbeing was phenomenal.

Deborah's story

Deborah was a middle-aged woman who came to see me for anxiety and depression. She was a very business-like conservative person. She told me her friend had been to see me and was doing extremely well. (Her friend was the previous client, John). I thought about Time Line Therapy for Deborah, but because of her rather stern, business-like manner I made the assumption that it wouldn't be right for her. Based on my past experience of dealing with certain personality types, I didn't think this woman would respond well to that particular type of therapy and that she would want what she came for – hypnotherapy. So, I decided not to use any other processes.

After our session she voiced that she was somewhat disappointed and had been hoping for Time Line Therapy because it had made such a difference to her friend's life.

I had let my assumptions and belief systems (my B.S.) about Deborah's personality type, get in the way of giving her what she actually wanted. In fact, if I'd asked the right questions about her expectations for her session, half the work would already have been done. She already believed that 'the technique I did with John' would work for her too.

Of course, I consequently adapted to meet her needs and expectations, and at the following session we did Time Line Therapy (with great success). Had she not expressed her feelings and simply left the first session disappointed; I may have never realized my mistake.

> *I had let my assumptions and belief systems (my B.S.) about Deborah's personality type, get in the way of giving her what she actually wanted.*

Now whether Deborah's success was because I met her expectations for a successful session and did Time Line Therapy, or whether she would have been able to achieve the same level of success with hypnotherapy or any other type of therapy is beside the point. The fastest route to her success was by understanding and meeting her expectations and her existing belief that Time Line Therapy technique would work. She already had evidence of that with John's results too.

Ensure your client understands their role – it's a partnership

Sometimes clients just want to be fixed. And they want the therapist to 'fix' them. (Whether it be a hypnotherapist, psychologist, counselor, life coach or any other modality).

As therapists, one of the first things we need to learn is that we do not or cannot 'fix' anyone. In truth, clients don't need 'fixing' because they are not 'broken,' they have just fallen off track or lost their balance and we help by facilitating the space for them to re-align.

In truth, clients don't need 'fixing' because they are not 'broken

In reality, however, the truth is that some people do actually feel like they are 'broken'. It is an important part of our job to help them realize that they are not broken, they are not weak, they have just lost their way and they can trust us to help lead them back to feeling safe and strong again.

Our role is to guide the client through a process that enables them to access the resources they already possess to move from their present state to their desired outcome.

I sometimes describe it to the client using this language,

"**I will take you by the hand and walk you through to the other side.**"

I know, and it's important that they know, that I cannot walk there **for them**, but if they are open to the process, and follow my instructions, we can do it together.

It seems simple enough and obvious enough to us as therapists, but if the client doesn't understand how to do that then achieving their outcome may not happen. Let's be honest, sometimes we've all made assumptions about the client's level of understanding or their expectations.

Kate's story

A new client, Kate, told me that she had previously had hypnotherapy and it didn't work at all. In my pretalk, I asked her a number of questions to clarify what happened:

- Did you feel safe and comfortable with the therapist and also throughout the session?

- Did you understand the process and do everything you were instructed by the hypnotherapist to do?

Kate replied, *"Absolutely. I lay on his couch and listened while he talked and when I woke up at the end, I left his office, but nothing changed."*

Before I complete Kate's story, this gives rise to an important question.

- If indeed Kate did fall asleep, instead of going into hypnosis, will the therapy still work? Or alternatively,

- If the client, 'completely zones out' during a session of counseling, psychology or other therapeutic model, will it still work? Further to that,

- What if the therapist doesn't have the skills to determine if the client has fallen asleep or 'zoned out'?

I know for certain, from my mentoring of therapists, that they sometimes feel that the client loses focus. If this means the client's mind has drifted off elsewhere, are they absorbing anything the therapist is saying?

I have asked many, many highly respected and renowned therapists these questions and the answers always vary considerably. Even the most prominent and experienced people in this field have different opinions.

- Some believe that the suggestions are still being integrated at some level, even though the client appears to have zoned out or fallen asleep.

- Others believe that if the client is 'not present' they will miss the entire therapeutic objective of the session and nothing will change.

- Others, like myself, believe we should always be testing the subconscious with ideomotor or sensory signals, to determine if the subconscious part of the mind is present and doing the work, because it is positive change through subconscious reprograming, we seek to achieve.

Either way, the client needs to understand how the process works, what to expect, what not to expect, and what their role in the treatment will be. And the therapist needs the skills to ascertain during the session whether the client is absorbing, accepting and responding to the suggestions and that, at least, **their subconscious is actively participating in the therapy**.

Kate's story continued:

In Kate's case,

- if her expectations of hypnosis had been gauged by the therapist before the hypnosis part of the session had begun, and

- if the therapist had debriefed Kate after her session

- both Kate and the therapist would have been able to address the discrepancy on the day. Kate would not have been left with a belief that 'hypnotherapy doesn't work.'

The client's role

The important thing to be aware of is that the client needs to actively fulfill their role within the therapy session. So, a great pretalk clearly outlines everything that the client needs to know and do in order to achieve a successful outcome. (In the appendix I've provided an example of the pretalk structure I use.)

Another aspect that is important for the client to have is a basic understanding of, (particularly in the case of hypnotherapy) the difference between the conscious processes of the mind and the unconscious processes of the mind. As I mentioned previously, most clients will seek therapy for issues over which they feel they have no conscious control because logically (consciously) they know what they want – but illogically (through past unconscious programming) they do the opposite. So, the client needs to understand which part of the mind we are working with specifically and what is the best way to communicate with that part of the mind.

Some people will have heard of the conscious and unconscious (or subconscious) mind and have a general idea of the concept, others will have an in-depth understanding which may or may not align with the therapist's viewpoint, while some will have never heard of these concepts.

What is important here, is that we talk to them about it, understand their viewpoint and offer some insights to align the client's expectations with what they are about to experience, without overwhelming them. (Our role is not to show how clever we are, but to open the doorway to just the right amount of information and structure that will help the client have a clear perspective of what to expect during the session.) This is also an important aspect of the therapeutic partnership that will ensure we are all on the same page and each do our part as we work together toward a successful outcome.

Our role is not to show how clever we are, but to open the doorway to just the right amount of information

---

While any descriptions of the conscious and unconscious mind are simply metaphors to describe our understanding of the workings of the mind, it is very clear that the deeper (unconscious), feeling part of the mind operates via a different criteria and makes decisions based on different factors than the logical, thinking (conscious) part of the mind. In many therapies the therapist is working with conscious processes (the conscious mind). In hypnotherapy we are working with deeper unconscious processes (the unconscious mind). Why is it important for the client to be aware of this? Because most habits and addictions, as well as other unconscious processes such as anxiety and depression, are based and triggered by the programming of the deeper unconscious part of the mind.

This means that they are automatic behaviors and responses and, as such, are often inevitably out of our conscious control. If the client understands how the different aspects of the mind work and how to work effectively with their own mind, they will be able to work effectually *with* you during the session and after it, rather than inadvertently working against the changes that they want to experience (for example, self-sabotage.)

It is my strong belief that every therapist needs to communicate with the different levels of the mind if we are to consistently achieve the greatest outcomes for our clients. There are many ways to do this.

Both the client and the therapist consciously want the same thing – amazing results. Our role as the therapist is to ensure we help the unconscious, automatic part of the mind to want that same result too.

It is my strong belief that every therapist needs to communicate with the different levels of the mind if we are to consistently achieve the greatest outcomes for our clients.

It is interesting to note that up until quite recent times, hypnotherapy was included in the standard training for doctors, dentists and psychologists and is still endorsed by most major medical associations in western society. The importance of working with the unconscious processes of the human mind has always been understood as an integral part of the healing process.

When we take the time to make sure the client is aware of their role in the process and committed to doing their part, both within the sessions and within the other parameters of their life, we help them achieve greater outcomes.

Kerry's story

I recently treated a young woman named Kerry. She came to me with severe anxiety and depression. She'd been self-harming and was suicidal. Kerry didn't actually want to talk to me. Her mother had brought her to the session against her will and asked me to 'fix' her before she killed herself.

When her mother made the appointment, she had told me not to let her daughter know that I was a hypnotherapist because if she knew, she would walk out.

Kerry was crying and angry when she arrived. She couldn't see a way out of her current situation. She had a broken leg and was feeling stuck in her current circumstances. She was living in an abusive environment, but the only other available option for her was going to her mother's house. This idea felt very uncomfortable for her because her stepdad was there. Her circumstances did indeed feel stuck.

After spending time listening to Kerry, building rapport and creating a safe space for her to express her feelings, I questioned further about why she didn't want to go to her mother's house, temporarily at least. Kerry confided that her stepdad was actually okay, she had never really had any major problem with him, but she just didn't feel comfortable moving in with him and her mum.

I asked her if it would be more uncomfortable than living in her current abusive environment.

One of the problems with living in trauma and high levels of stress is that the body and mind are in 'shut down survival' mode which means that we don't easily access logical thinking.

- Consciously, Kerry needed to escape her current situation (almost to the point of committing suicide)
- Unconsciously, however, Kerry was stuck in 'fight, flight, freeze' mode and she was literally 'frozen' in her fear and despair'.

These processes need to be resolved before any real change can happen.

It was imperative that she remove herself from her current environment, but her logical thought processes had shut down and she was stuck – even though there was a clear way out and she had support from her family. I have often heard therapists, family members and friends of people who live in abusive situations desperately frustrated with the failure of their client or loved one to accept the help that is available to them. From the outside it appears that the person is sabotaging their own wellbeing and destroying any hope of a safe and happy life. Underneath, there are unconscious processes keeping them stuck. These processes need to be resolved before any real change can happen.

Kerry's story continued
It took time, but eventually Kerry felt safe with me. We established a comfortable, genuine rapport and she agreed that working with me would be helpful.

I helped Kerry understand that she had to take some major steps to help herself and that if she remained in her current environment, the trauma she was experiencing would keep her desperately stuck and prevent her recovery.

I also explained that if I were to help her, she must do everything she could to help herself so that, together, we could put all of this behind her and create something wonderful, a new life. I built enough rapport with Kerry at a conscious and unconscious level to make her feel safe with me. Once she felt safe, we established trust. We then did hypnotherapy to help her feel stronger at an unconscious level so that she had clarity and the strength of mind to do what she needed to do at a conscious level.

When she returned for her second session, Kerry had listened to every word I had previously said and had taken the necessary actions. She had moved in with her mum temporarily and it was going amazingly well. Her stepdad made her feel very welcome and protected. She had spoken to her closest friend about getting an apartment together, the friend had agreed, and they had even found the perfect place.

When Kerry came in for her third session, she had already moved into the new apartment, broken leg and all, and felt happy and optimistic about her future. She was returning to work earlier than anticipated and had great support from her workplace to take on lighter duties because of her broken leg.

By fully engaging in the sessions, thus working at both the conscious and unconscious levels of the mind, and taking the necessary actions to change her environment, Kerry had been able to move from the emotional freeze and take the steps to free herself from her abusive circumstances. She had been able to separate her fear about her current emotional abuse from the potential haven that was being offered to her by her mother and stepfather. She had changed her life one step at a time. I didn't fix her, I provided a safe place to help her address the present reality, find clarity, release the unconscious fear that had kept her 'frozen' and then take the conscious steps and actions to literally change her life from inescapable desperation to fabulous. Together we performed a little bit of magic.

That outcome happened because Kerry:

1. Felt safe with me

2. Felt heard by me

3. Built a relationship of trust with me

Together we performed a little bit of magic.

She came to believe that I could help her because I empathized with her, took the time to understand her needs and coached her to understand her part in the solution. She also understood that I couldn't fix her situation, she needed to be the one to take action, but I could help her resolve the unconscious processes that stopped her from taking the necessary actions to ensure her own safety and wellbeing.

How we achieved these objectives

Because Kerry was living in an abusive environment, the part of her brain responsible for survival was constantly on high alert keeping her in 'fight, flight, freeze' mode. This meant her body was continuously flooded with adrenaline and other stress hormones. Her emotional state was preventing her from thinking clearly and was keeping her stuck in shut down survival mode. Little wonder she was suicidal. Her traumatic circumstances and emotional state were creating havoc with her biology through an overload of stress hormones surging through her body. She was caught in a cycle and could see no way out; her physiology was keeping her stuck there.

- ☐ My first goal was to connect with Kerry by showing empathy, and for her to feel understood, heard and safe with me so that we could effectively work together.
- ☐ My second goal was to use hypnosis to unconsciously get her out of 'fight, flight, freeze mode' and bring her emotional state and her biology back into balance. It is almost impossible to work logically with anyone until they click off 'emergency alert' mode and return to a state of homeostasis and clarity. The quickest and most effective way to achieve this is through hypnosis.
- ☐ My third goal was to have her accept her role in the therapeutic relationship, 'step up' and take the necessary actions to escape her abusive environment so she could feel safe in her everyday life.
- ☐ My final goal was for her to move into the future with effective strategies to deal with life's future situations confidently and competently.

Many clients state very clearly what they don't want and have trouble voicing what it is they do want

The way we start out will determine the way we finish.

If we start out without rapport and aligned expectations and goals, a session is far more likely to end without the results both you and the client want.

Always ask the client what they want to achieve from the sessions. Many therapists focus on the 'problem' or 'issue'. They want to diagnoze and label their 'patient'. Many clients state very clearly what they don't want and have trouble voicing what it is they do want. The client needs to be very clear on what they want from the therapy. Only then is it possible to ascertain whether the therapy has been successful in achieving the desired outcome.

In the next chapter we'll delve deeper into setting up your client for success.

Remember to download your free
'What to Do When What You Did Didn't Work' resources
www.therapistshandbook.com/resources

Sometimes we create our own failures through the picture in our head of how it's supposed to be."

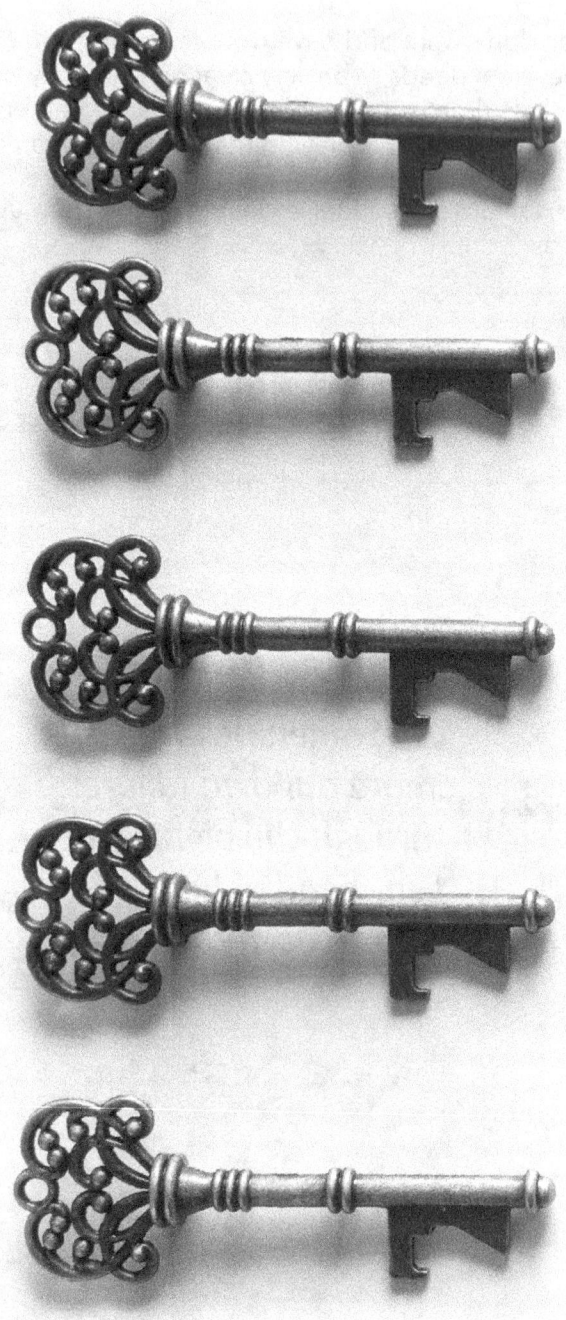

CHAPTER 2

The 5 Keys to Set Your Client Up For Success

> *"The key factor for success is believing you can do it and believing it will work."*
>
> *Leonie O'Connell*

Setting up the client, and congruently the therapist, for success is imperative to the session and the outcome. One of my favorite sayings is, "Your success is my success."

Let's face it, we are in this together with our clients.

Setting the session up for a successful outcome does not have to be complex, nor is it difficult.

Once you have met the client and established genuine rapport, it's as easy as:

A B C D E.

The 5 Keys to Success	
A	ALIGN
B	BELIEVE
C	CLARIFY
D	DECIDE
E	EXPLAIN

Let's understand this further:

ALIGN

Ensure the therapist and the client have the same goals, expectations and beliefs about what will happen. Never let the client's or the therapist's B.S. (belief systems) get in the way of a great outcome.

> ### Rose's Story
>
> Several years ago, I worked with Rose, who was an elderly woman with chronic back pain. When she came to see me, Rose explained that she had done her research. She knew that pain is the brain's way of warning the body that there is an immediate danger present which requires attention. She knew that this response was not necessarily a true indication of what was happening in the body. And she knew that there was no immediate danger in her body because she had been to doctors and had X-rays and scans. Rose explained, *"Apart from some normal arthritic changes that come with age, I am healthy and there is no organic reason for the pain to still exist."*
>
> Rose explained that she understood the 'what' and the 'why', and all she needed from me was the 'how'. She knew what was happening in her physiology, and why she was experiencing her pain. She just needed me to facilitate the 'how' so she could eliminate it.

At that point early in my career, I wasn't so sure that she could *completely eliminate* her pain. She, however, had a total belief in her body's ability to release this pain.

I knew I couldn't work with her unless I had the skills, the techniques and, most importantly, the belief that she could achieve her goal. I knew that I had to be able to align my goals and beliefs with hers if we were to have success. I knew that we were out of alignment and I should refer her to another therapist.

> *We had aligned goals and beliefs and achieved a great outcome.*

The problem was that at that point in my career, I didn't know who I could possibly refer her to. So, I became determined to do my research in order to help me believe being pain free was possible. I sought the knowledge and skills required to achieve this goal. I developed a program of four sessions, and I felt certain we could have Rose living comfortably in her own body.

I gained the proficiencies. I aligned my expectations with hers and by the time we entered into the sessions, I had total belief in her ability to live comfortably in her own body. And together we quickly achieved it. We had aligned goals and beliefs and achieved a great outcome. Alignment is intricately interwoven with the next point – 'believe'.

BELIEVE

Believe that the client will absolutely achieve their outcome.

Never work with a client if you don't believe that they can achieve the outcome they seek. (Or change your belief by educating yourself about the possibilities.)

It is equally important to ensure that the client also believes that they can achieve their desired outcome.

I am the co-founder and principal instructor of The Academy of Therapeutic Hypnosis. We teach people processes that are tried and tested to achieve outstanding results. I believe in teaching my students advanced techniques that are highly effective and easily replicable. Our Quit Smoking process is a transformative approach that many of our graduates have used as the foundation to create their extremely successful hypnotherapy practices.

> *They believe. I believe. Therefore, we are already 80% of the way to a successful outcome before the session even commences. I simply need to take them the other 20% with my protocol.*

One of my graduates told me that she had transformed the Quit Smoking process into an entirely new and different five-step process. When I asked her why, she told me that she knew all along that the technique I taught couldn't possibly work and, in actual fact, it didn't work well at all when she used it.

What she did was actualize her own belief that this technique wouldn't work. She was entering her sessions with the belief that the process wouldn't work and that became her reality. Yet, for every other hypnotherapist I have trained who totally believed in this process, the success rates are astounding. Graduates have built six-figure businesses that start with the foundation of our quit smoking protocol.

When I work with clients to help them quit smoking, 90% of my clientele book through word of mouth. They actually know someone who has quit cigarettes due to attending a session with me. This has an amazing impact on the session and the success rate because they come to me with total belief that this works. They believe. I believe. Therefore, we are already 80% of the way to a successful outcome before the session even commences. I simply need to take them the other 20% with my protocol.

When I work with clients who have come to me through an online search or through avenues other than 'word of mouth', they are often quite skeptical about hypnotherapy and the claim that they can quit smoking easily after just one session. My initial role is to have them overcome their skepticism and instill the belief that they can, and will, be successful. It is imperative to **align** our **belief** in the process before we even begin. But if I have not determined their level of skepticism in my pretalk, how can I possibly address this?

CLARIFY

Be clear on your client's expectations, beliefs and values.

Never assume that the client has the same expectations, beliefs and values as the therapist. Never assume that what you expect for the client aligns with their expectations.

Sandra's story

I recently worked with Sandra, who had extreme anxiety issues related to past abuse. She was suffering PTSD (Post Traumatic Stress Disorder) and she requested a particular therapy model in which I was qualified. It's a very specific process for PTSD that is highly effective in treating trauma related issues such as anxiety and depression.

Because she had researched and requested this specific process, I *assumed* that she had a good understanding of what was involved.

Part of this process involved working with anger. We did this session and the following week, Sandra reported that her anxiety levels had not changed. I went over the events of the previous session with her, where we had dealt with the unresolved anger and helplessness from her past experiences, and she reported that she hadn't followed my instructions for that session. She had ignored my suggestions and had done the process in her own way. Sandra then told me she had specific spiritual beliefs and that she refused to 'do anger'. She was only prepared to work with forgiveness and tolerance. She insisted that she had no anger, only compassion and that's how she always approached her issues. What she expected from our sessions was to focus on forgiveness. That was what she always did and that was what she wanted now.

I explained to her that if what she was already doing (forgiveness and compassion) wasn't working, then a new approach could be exactly what she needed. Sandra confirmed she had been working using the 'forgiveness model' for many years and was still suffering severe anxiety. She agreed she still felt like a victim to her past trauma. She felt that if she could forgive the perpetrator, she would find peace and resolve her anxiety and depression. Her problem was that this 'forgiveness' strategy wasn't working for her at all. The process she had requested used an entirely different approach which she'd subsequently decided she wasn't prepared to engage in.

I had seen numerous remarkable results from clients who have been able to deal with the helplessness of their past situation and empower themselves using this technique by addressing subconscious, repressed anger. I informed Sandra that when they did this, their anxiety disappeared almost miraculously. She refused to participate in this process any longer and demanded a refund.

My mistake was that because she had requested this particular course of treatment, I assumed she understood what was involved. I hadn't clarified the process with her during the pretalk, or prior to the sessions, therefore I was not clear on her values, beliefs and expectations.

Had I clarified her understanding of that treatment model right at the outset, we would have identified this mismatch and, if she was still unwilling to use that approach, I would have opted for an entirely different therapy model that would have resonated with Sandra's values. As it turned out, the lack of clarity and the miscommunication led to a situation where neither Sandra nor I achieved a successful outcome.

> *Had I clarified her understanding of that treatment model right at the outset, we would have identified this mismatch and, if she was still unwilling to use that approach, I would have opted for an entirely different therapy model that would have resonated with Sandra's values.*

DECIDE

Decide on a course of action and whether or not you are the right therapist to truly help this client.

Recognize and accept if you are not the best therapist for the client's current needs. Never question or try to alter your client's values. If you are uncomfortable with accepting their values, morals or ethics while being able to remain true to yourself, refer them to someone who can. If you don't believe that you can authentically and effectively provide the therapeutic approach that the client requests, refer them to someone who can.

It's rare, but occasionally I meet with a client and, for one reason or another, I don't feel 'right' about working with them. Perhaps it's because I don't believe that this is the right therapy modality for them or because I don't truly believe that I am the right person to lead them to their desired outcome.

Perhaps it's because I don't believe that they are ready for the therapy or this is not the right time for them to create the change they're seeking. Perhaps I just couldn't create the level of rapport that I believe is necessary for an effective and positive outcome, or my values just didn't align with theirs and I couldn't be congruent with helping them achieve their desired outcome.

> *It really doesn't matter what the reason is, if we sense that it just doesn't feel right, do the thing that is of highest good for the client and yourself.*

It's extremely important to recognize when the therapy you offer is not right for this person at this time, or you are not the right person to work with this client at this time … AND … it's fundamental that you decide not to work with this person, and have the integrity to say so.

Of course, it's vitally important to be able to refer this person to a therapist who can help them. We should never make anyone feel like we are rejecting them. We should always come from a caring space and let the client know that we believe in their ability to overcome their current difficulties, but we want to refer them to a therapist who is a specialist in that field or better equipped to help them.

Amanda's story

I treated Amanda, a young woman who had experienced significant trauma. We successfully worked together and afterwards she confided in me that at the age of forty, she had never had sexual intercourse.

Despite having been in a long-term relationship with a man, she could never submit to having sex. It was a breakthrough for her to confide in me, but I knew I wasn't the best therapist to help her with this issue. I referred her to a specialist who treated patients for all challenges related to sex. The therapist was very experienced, and I knew that because of the trust and rapport Amanda and I had built, she would accept my recommendation. It was a great decision and Amanda contacted me after her treatment, to say thank you for my help.

Mark's story

Mark came to see me to quit smoking. He was a barrister and was quite obviously anxious and visibly shaky during our initial discussion. I asked him what medications he was taking and discovered he was on a cocktail of different medications for anxiety and depression. He told me that he had done several quit smoking programs and none of them had worked. I congratulated him, because he was here to see me, and it showed his determination to succeed. Mark said, *"I'm desperate and I don't know what I will do if I fail again."*

On further questioning, I knew that until Mark received help for his current mental health challenges, he would most likely be triggered to fall back on to cigarettes again. I was concerned that 'failing' again would further damage his mental health, so I explained to him that the quit smoking session he wanted was not, as yet, the correct solution for him. He had become attached to smoking as his 'anxiety relief' and if he tried to quit without first addressing the anxiety, he would be very likely to give in to the need to smoke again.

> *Unfortunately, Mark wasn't yet prepared to work on the deeper issues. As for me, I did the right thing for Mark by not working with him until he was ready.*

I explained that, in his eyes, this would constitute yet another failure. We needed to work with the anxiety and other underlying issues causing the depression first, and when that was dealt with, we could then focus on quitting smoking.

Mark chose not to do that and left my office in the same state he came in. I strongly suggested that he seek help from his doctor or other mental health professional and made recommendations.

I would have dearly loved to help him, but the truth is, I knew engaging in a quit smoking session was not the right thing to do for Mark. At this point in time it could have done more harm than good. There were far more important challenges he needed to overcome, and I genuinely felt that there was a danger of him plummeting into deeper depression and escalating his anxiety if we did the quit smoking session and he 'failed' yet again. Unfortunately, Mark wasn't yet prepared to work on the deeper issues. As for me, I did the right thing for Mark by not working with him until he was ready.

EXPLAIN

Make sure your client understands that every therapy is a 'do with you' process, not a 'do to you' process.

No matter what modality you work with, managing the client's expectations right from the outset is a key component of a successful treatment plan.

Help the client understand that, as the therapist,

- You can only do your part
- The client must do their part as well, and
- Never assume that the client understands the process and how it works.
- Never let the client believe that their recovery or healing is your responsibility.

Any therapist can only guide their clients to their desired outcomes. The client must be an active and willing participant committed to their own wellbeing. It's a partnership and this needs to be explained and clearly understood.

Sometimes in our eagerness to be 'everything for everyone' we forget that we are only half of the equation.

Sam's story

Some time ago I worked with a young man who had a challenge with marijuana use. His life had spiraled out of control. He had a partner and a child but no longer lived with them. He lived in a small apartment his parents had built for him at the back of their house. He had what could only be described as a volatile relationship with everyone. He had a lot of anger, couldn't hold down a job and had been responsible for several car accidents.

Despite the fact (or perhaps because of the fact) that his parents had done so much for him, giving him everything they could to care for him and look after him, his life was a mess.

He wasn't engaging in the therapy and our sessions were not going well. I knew that I had to break his pattern of reliance. He blamed everyone else for his problems and I knew if he didn't address this, he would stay in the same recurring patterns until he did.

When it was quite clear to me that we weren't achieving anything, I decided to try a bit of a 'shock' tactic'. What I did wasn't shocking at all, but I think being spoken to quite bluntly, actually did shock Sam. He was used to everyone 'treading on egg shells' around him to avoid upsetting him or creating yet another argument.

Step one:

I explained to Sam that I couldn't 'fix' him, but more importantly that it wasn't my responsibility to fix him or his life. I held my hands out together to form a cup shape in front of him which provided a visual representation of what I was about to say.

Step two:

I told him to pretend that in my hands was his life, his future. I asked him to pretend that I held the responsibility for his life, his future right there in the palms of my hands. And then I asked him, *"Sam, what should I do with your life? What if I choose to just throw it in the bin because I have more important things to think about? What happens to your life then?"*

He sat silently and was visibly annoyed by my metaphor. I continued, *"Who should be holding this and taking care of it? This is your life! Who is responsible for how it turns out? Do you really think it's my responsibility? Do you think it is your parent's responsibility? Do you really want to be leaving it in the hands of everyone else?"*

Step three:

And then I said quite sternly, *"I can tell you one thing for sure, I wouldn't be letting anyone else hold onto the responsibility for my life. I would never put my life in anyone else's hands. It's far too precious for that. My life is far more valuable to me than it is to anyone else, so why would I ever allow such a thing?"*

I took his silence as permission to continue, *"It's time for you to step up and take responsibility for what's happening in your life. You're the only one who can do that. And if you don't do it soon, things are just going to keep spiraling out of control and no-one is going to be able to stop it. It all comes down to you!!!"*

Step four:

After a short silence, I changed my voice to a gentler, kinder tone and said, *"Come on. Let's work together. We both want the same thing. I can't do this for you, but we can definitely do it together."*

It was a risky strategy, but it was also a perfect 'pattern interruption'. I needed to connect with him on a meaningful level and up until now he had been very resistant. Connection and 'partnership' in working toward his success hadn't happened thus far.

I had tried everything else up until that point. I had to accept that he might get angry and walk out, but if it worked, he might have an important realization. The chance of a positive shift was worth the risk.

Sam's story continued

The importance of silence
Sam sat silent for a few moments and I simply gave him space and held the silence waiting patiently for his response. I could almost see the cogs winding around in his brain as he moved from disbelief to resistance to acceptance. YES!! Acceptance and empowerment. This was the turning point in our therapy and in Sam's life.

I've talked a lot about client expectations in the first two chapters and how they can derail your best intentions. In Chapter 3 we'll dive deeper into how you can help your clients believe that the outcome they are working towards is possible.

> Remember to download your free
> *'What to Do When What You Did Didn't Work'* resources
> www.therapistshandbook.com/resources

"The Key factor for success is believing you can do it and believing it will work."

CHAPTER 3

Great Expectations – Whose Are They Anyway?

"Pause the wheels of your mind and know that your intuition is greater than any obstacle you will come up against."

John O'Connell

What does the client really expect from the therapy and why does it matter?

It's important to be certain that the client believes they can actualize their goal and that they trust you, as the therapist, to take them there.

Even more importantly, it is vital to ensure that you understand what their expectations are and align your expectations with theirs. Sometimes, as therapists, we want and expect much more for our client than they hope for themselves.

Sometimes we are far more optimistic about our client's possible outcomes than they are. It becomes so important to us that we get a great outcome for them, that we can lose sight of the fact that the client must expect and believe in the same result as the therapist for this to happen.

It's possible that when a client comes to see you for a certain challenge and you ask them what they want to achieve from the therapy, you could misinterpret their description of their expectations.

The most important aspect of any therapy is to listen – truly listen to what your client is saying without making assumptions.

Shelley's story

Some time ago, Shelley came to see me for chronic pain. She had interstitial cystitis and had suffered discomfort ranging from uncomfortable tenderness to excruciating pain every day for almost 30 years. She had tried drugs and cortisone treatments; she had even had surgical implants for pain management. Every treatment had resulted in further injury, side effects and increased levels of discomfort and she now felt a sense of hopelessness about her future.

When I asked her what she wanted to achieve from our work together, she said, *"I just want to try and deal with this excruciating pain."*

At the time, my interpretation of what she said was, she hoped to eliminate the pain.
Her interpretation was that she wanted to be able to cope with the pain so that it was manageable and no longer excruciating.

During our third session, Shelley informed me that during the last week she had been totally pain free for the first time in 30 years and she remained pain free for four consecutive days. She said she'd spent the entire four days cleaning her house, emptying out closets, rearranging furniture and basically working flat-out to get as much as possible done before the pain returned. She was terrified that after the pain disappeared so suddenly, her agony would be even more unbearable when it returned.

On the fifth day she awoke with the 'familiar' excruciating pain.

I asked her why she believed the pain would return after all the work we had done to free her from it. She appeared confused by the question.

"I can never be free of this pain, Leonie" she said. "My doctors have made it very clear that I must learn how to live with it and manage it. I will have it for the rest of my life, and nothing can be done about that. The fact that it went away for a few days was very strange and incredibly wonderful, but I knew with absolute certainty it would return."

"So why did you come to me?" I asked.

"To learn how to manage it", she responded. *"Not to get rid of it. That can't happen."*

"But it did happen", I explained. *"And if you can be pain free for four full days, you can be pain free for a week, and a month, and a year, then for the rest of your life."*

"Oh, Leonie," she responded, *"that would mean that for the last 30 years all the doctors I've seen and all the pain clinics I've been to would have to be wrong. And that's simply not possible, surely. No, I just need to learn how to manage this pain better than I've been able to in the past, because I just can't keep on living like this."*

Lesson learned.

The client cannot achieve an outcome that they don't believe is possible or, as yet, are not willing to consider a change in belief.

One big lesson that I took from this experience was that I had not clearly understood the client's expectations right from the outset. I had presumed my expectations and treated her according to my beliefs, not considering hers.

Nor had I aligned her expectations with my own.

- ☐ Shelley had initially explained that she had come to me to try and deal with the pain she had lived with for so many years.
- ☐ My interpretation was that she wanted to free herself from pain.
- ☐ My belief was that she could become pain free and live comfortably in her own body.
- ☐ Her interpretation was that she might be able to manage her pain better. Her belief was that she could never be free of it.

And until Shelley believed that she could, she would not achieve a different outcome.

> The client and therapist must believe that the outcome they are working toward is possible. Clients will not actualize what they do not believe is possible for them. Clients will not actualize what the therapist does not believe is possible for them.
>
> So are your beliefs, and your client's beliefs aligned?
> Are you both expecting limited or unlimited outcomes?

Win-Win Outcomes

The secret formula to align client and therapist expectations and beliefs

The magic formula for success is			
Rapport	+ Respect	+ Expertise	+ Creativity
Equals a little bit of magic!			

Rapport

This is the first and most important step. Having a good rapport is not just a superficial, friendly interaction. It's not a hierarchal professional affiliation where the therapist is somewhat superior. And it's not a series of strategies that you use to create some artificial form of communication.

> *Having rapport means that there is a genuine connection.*

Having rapport means that there is a genuine connection. Your client believes they are in caring, safe hands. They feel heard and understood and there is an easy flow to the communication. The therapist genuinely instils trust through empathy, warmth and care. You may be the most skilled person in your profession, but when it comes to therapy, the client needs to feel the connection before they can fully engage in the process. Only then can there be genuine trust in the therapist and the process.

Paula's story.

Paula had been seeing a psychologist for several months to work through mental health challenges. Her psychologist suggested that the underlying cause of all her difficulties was past trauma and Paula knew it was true. When she came to see me, Paula was ready to confront and release the emotional issues attached to her trauma. She didn't want to do this with her psychologist, even though she had already done so much work with her.

When I asked Paula why, she told me, *"My psychologist is very good at what she does, but I just don't feel like I can do this with her. She's very professional but also impersonal. I wouldn't feel comfortable."*

She also confided that she had been to three other therapists in search of someone she could feel comfortable with and I was the right person.

- ☐ Firstly, and most importantly, Paula needed to find someone that she could trust and connect with on a softer, more sensitive level.
- ☐ Secondly, she had to believe that the therapist had the skills and knowledge to help her. Only then could she engage in the treatment.

> *While a genuine rapport is crucial, your client is not your friend.*

Respect

While a genuine rapport is crucial, your client is not your friend. This is a person-centered professional relationship built not only on trust, but also on respect. Beneath that sense of empathy, connection and trust is a sense of professional regard where the client values your professionalism and has confidence in your expertise.

Candace's story

Candace was a young woman brought to me by her mother. She was clearly resistant to being in my office and was quite unresponsive to my attempts to interact with her.
In her frustration, she asked, *"Can we just get this over with as quickly as possible? I need a smoke."*

I responded in a very even, unperturbed tone, *"Sure. Our appointment is over. Off you go."*

Much to my surprise, her reply was quite indignant, *"Don't you dare tell me to leave, you haven't done anything. We've paid you good money."* To which I calmly responded, *"I'm sorry, Candace, but I have a huge waiting list of people who want to be helped. You haven't paid me anything yet and I have no intention of taking up your smoking time trying to convince you to let me help you. There will be no charge for this consultation."*

On that note her mother said, *"I'm leaving."* And as she left my office she told her daughter, *"Make up your mind what you want to do and don't waste any more of Leonie's valuable time."*

Candace defiantly stated, *"I came here for a reason and I am not leaving."*

I knew this was an opportune moment to start the rapport building process all over again. In her mind, Candace had turned the situation around and it was no longer her mother's decision to be here, it was Candace's choice. This was an empowering moment for her.

I had set my professional boundaries and gained her respect. Now I needed to turn the situation around to create a harmonious partnership to commence our work together. The therapy may have had a rocky beginning, but the end results were phenomenal.

Creativity & expertise

When you first start out in your career you will have your own set of values and beliefs, life experiences and a certain level of qualification. Expertise comes with training and experience, and creativity comes with imagination and inventiveness. When you mix your expertise and capability with a touch of creativity, you can produce a unique therapy experience for each and every client based on their needs, their individuality and their life experiences. This will allow them to move from their current level of understanding and resourcefulness to their positive outcome. And very often, especially when the client has been very stuck in their issue, it can seem like you've performed a little bit of magic.

When you mix your expertise and capability with a touch of creativity, you can produce a unique therapy experience for each and every client based on their needs, their individuality and their life experiences.

Don't treat your client like a client

Every client is a person with strengths and vulnerabilities, hopes and dreams, a past, a present and a future, just like you. It's easy to focus on your client as an 'issue' rather than as a whole person with many facets.

There has been extensive research dating back to 1974 done on the effectiveness of therapy for clients and the factors that determine the outcomes of different therapies with different clients.

The research has included several different therapy modalities and concluded that the overriding determining factor to the success of the therapy was the therapist. It wasn't the type of therapy or the modality – it was the therapist.

The research concluded that within the scope of 100 different therapeutic treatment approaches, the therapist was the determining factor as to how successful the therapy was in achieving the desired outcome for the client.[1] There is also research evidence demonstrating that when prescription medication is combined with therapy, the effectiveness of the medication is directly affected by the quality of the therapist. According to research quoted by Scott D. Miller from the International Centre for Clinical Excellence, *"Drugs used in combination with talk therapy were ten times more effective with the best therapists than with the worst therapists."*

Given this research and the findings that the best therapists can be ten times more effective, it's of vital importance to you, your business and your clients that you become the best therapist you can possibly be.

We've discussed the pretalk, empathy, creativity, rapport and the alignment of beliefs, but even when we apply all these skills to a session, we might still encounter blocks and problems.

In the following chapter I have provided a number of specific steps to go through and solutions to use when a client says, "It didn't work."

Remember to download your free
'What to Do When What You Did Didn't Work' resources
www.therapistshandbook.com/resources

---

[1] Miller, S.D., Hubble, M.A., & Duncan, B.L. (November/December, 2007). Supershrinks: Learning from the field's most effective practitioners. The Psychotherapy Networker, 31(6), 26-35, 56.

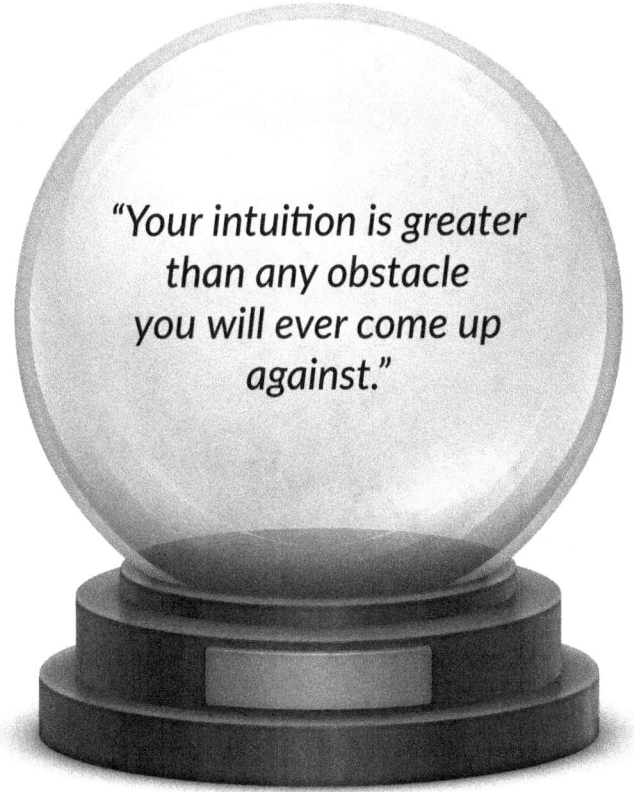

"Your intuition is greater than any obstacle you will ever come up against."

CHAPTER 4

What to Do When the Client Says, "It didn't work."

"Every problem can be understood if you ask the right questions."

John O'Connell

The quality of your questions will determine the quality of the outcome.

- Is it the client?
- Is it the therapist?

It's time to take a deeper look at your effectiveness and connect with your heart centre, not your ego.

Firstly, the client may not voice their feelings about their response (or lack of response) to their therapy if they haven't been asked the right questions. If the client is a 'nice person' who doesn't like to voice a negative opinion, they may not be totally honest with you about their progress unless they are given the opportunity to express their feelings in the way they feel comfortable.

If the therapist really wants to know the truth, they may need to dig a little deeper in a gentle, non-accusatory way to be able to delve into the truth of the situation. Asking general questions like, *"How are you going?"* may get a polite response rather than an honest one. Asking very pointed questions may make the client feel defensive and put them on edge.

Having a discussion where information is shared freely, while framing the conversation to uncover the truth of what is going on for the client, will always be more effective. But you must listen for clues. Be open. Ask the client what it is that they need. Questions need to be designed to elicit the sharing of information from a safe space. The therapist needs to listen with an open mind and an open heart.

But you must listen for clues.

Generally, when the client feels that it didn't work, they will be reluctant to say so. This may be because they don't have the level of rapport to be able to express their true feelings or it could be that they don't want to feel like a failure. Perhaps they don't want to feel as if they've let their therapist down or they are just waiting for the improvements to materialize even though they're not happening yet. These are often the clients who will simply stop coming and you will never know why.

If a client says it didn't work, the therapist will generally ask a range of questions to determine why. And remember, no-one is looking to point fingers or place blame. The therapist and the client want the same thing – a highly successful outcome.

When a client says it didn't work, the therapist needs to determine, without ego, a number of things about the client and about themselves as the therapist.

The client

1. Did the client fully engage?
2. Did the client have clarity around their own expectations and what they wanted to achieve from the therapy?
3. Did the client commit to the process and accept responsibility for their role in their own healing?
4. Did the client trust you and truly believe in you and your level of expertise?
5. Did the client follow all the instructions and follow through with any tasks that you asked them to complete between sessions?
6. Does the client need an entirely different approach?
7. Is there a benefit for the client if they stay stuck in their issue?
8. Why is this client still stuck?

Sometimes we need to turn the perspective around and find a different approach or viewpoint. What questions is the therapist asking him or herself?

Perhaps it's the therapist who's stuck? Or perhaps the therapist is empathizing with the client's doubts, fears or stuck feelings and failing to connect as cleanly as they need to get the best results. Perhaps the therapist is the one who is limited. This is not an accusatory statement; it is an opportunity to reflect on the entire process and be inspired to find new solutions that benefit everyone.

Perhaps it's the therapist who's stuck? Or perhaps the therapist is empathizing with the client's doubts, fears or stuck feelings and failing to connect as cleanly as they need to get the best results.

The therapist

1. Did your expectations align with your clients'?

2. Did you listen with an open mind and an open heart and tailor an approach for this client that was personal – or was the technique you engaged in a standardized approach that didn't work in this instance?

3. Did your beliefs about the expected outcomes align with the client's?

4. Did you bring any preconceived judgments, doubts or fears to the session?

5. Did you clarify if the client has preconceived judgments, doubts or fears?

6. Did you have genuine rapport? Does the client trust and feel safe with you?

7. Is there secondary or tertiary gain at play here?

8. Have you fully explored ways to engage the client's own resourcefulness?

9. Have you been creative and explored new approaches?

10. What have you missed?

If what you have done so far hasn't worked, have you ensured you've uncovered all potential secondary and tertiary gains? In the following chapter we'll go through specific steps and therapeutic ideas to do this, however, in the meantime we need to look at all possibilities.

Consider asking the client these questions:
1. What do you gain by staying the same?
2. What do you lose by staying the same?
3. What do you lose by changing?
4. What do you gain by changing?

The following questions seem to be along the same path, however, the small shift in the phrasing and intent can often reveal secondary gains that are close to consciousness.

1. What will happen if I do achieve this outcome?
2. What will happen if I don't?
3. What are the positive benefits of achieving this outcome?
4. What are the benefits of not achieving this outcome?
5. What are the negative consequences of achieving this outcome?
6. What are the negative consequences of not achieving this outcome?
7. How will I benefit if I don't achieve this outcome?
8. How will I benefit if I do achieve this outcome?

There are many other variations on these kinds of questions, the point is to 'confuse' the subconscious and potentially trip it up into bringing a secondary gain to the surface. Ask the client to just tell you the first thing that pops into their mind, to try not to think about the answers, simply speak the first thing that flows. Be sure to inform the client that if nothing flows, then that's okay too, simply tell them to say, "*Nothing comes to mind.*"

Positive purpose

A third line of questioning for the subconscious is:

If my subconscious had a positive purpose for holding onto this (challenge), what would it be?

Secondary gains, conscious or unconscious, are possibly the most common reason for the client staying stuck in their problem or issue.

> ### Ian's story
>
> I had been working with Ian's wife to help her solve past trauma issues which were causing her to experience anxiety, depression and marital problems. At his wife's request, Ian came to see me as well, in the hope of resolving the current relationship issues within the marriage. Long after our sessions would normally have been completed, Ian was still making regular appointments. I was concerned that even though he seemed to me to be making progress, and his wife believed that all was well, Ian still felt there was a lot of work to be done. It was, however, difficult for him to express what it was that he felt he still needed to work on.
>
> I was running out of ideas with Ian and decided that it was time to dig deeper and discover what was really going on with him. What was I missing?

This is what I discovered by asking the series of questions previously mentioned in the chapter.

Ian believed he had more to achieve by continuing to come and see me. His own mental and emotional wellbeing had improved significantly and his relationship with his wife was better than it had been in years. However, he felt that one of the major factors at play was that his wife was much more loving toward him because she felt so appreciative and supported by the fact that he was prepared to come and work with me. She was deeply touched that he was willing to resolve his own issues as a means to improving their relationship. He was afraid that when our sessions stopped, his wife would revert to feeling unsupported and things may deteriorate between them again.

We did a session to enhance Ian's confidence and strengthen the belief that he and his wife now have the skills, techniques and understanding to be able to move forward together, maintain the harmony in their relationship and deal with any issues as they arise.

On one level, both Ian and I had something to gain by allowing the sessions to continue. He had the perceived benefit of the belief that his wife would remain more loving toward him while he was attending therapy, and I had the potential benefit of simply accepting an easy stream of appointments from a paying customer even though I felt that continued therapy was not required. In fact, it may well have become detrimental to Ian if his belief that continuing to see me was necessary to maintain a happy marital status.

At the time of writing this book, it is over two years ago since I saw Ian and his wife, and I recently learned that they are still doing fabulously well.

As we've seen, Ian's secondary gain for remaining in therapy resulted in a *conscious* choice to continue. In the next chapter, I'll explore some scenarios where secondary gain was an *unconscious* response which was out of the client's conscious awareness. I'll also discuss how to recognize when there is an unconscious secondary gain and how to uncover and resolve those gains.

Remember to download your free
'What to Do When What You Did Didn't Work' resources
www.therapistshandbook.com/resources

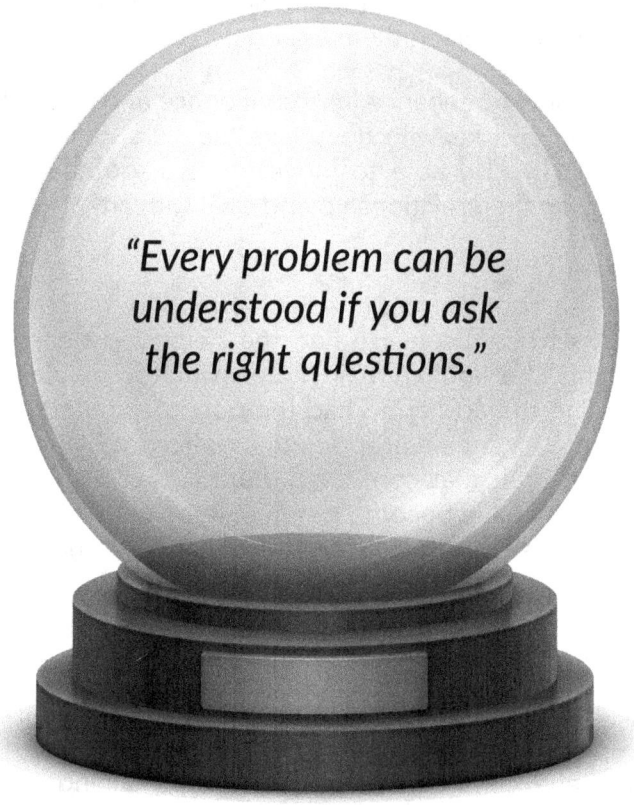

"Every problem can be understood if you ask the right questions."

CHAPTER 5

Identify and Eliminate Secondary and Tertiary Gains

"You are not stuck. You are just thinking the same thoughts, maintaining the same beliefs, speaking the same words, and doing the same things."

John O'Connell

The unconscious part of the mind reacts, responds and makes decisions based on a very different dynamic than the conscious mind.

Unconscious secondary gain is an attempt by the unconscious mind to keep the person safe, to care for and protect that person from a past traumatic memory or emotional reaction happening again.

The deepest foundation of human nature is to avoid pain and seek pleasure. When we have experienced something in life that moved us toward pain, our brain is pre-programmed to protect us from experiencing it again. It initiates a reaction or habit that alleviates the discomfort or suffering. This can happen at any time throughout our life. During childhood, certain feelings or experiences initiate unconscious programming that sets us up for life.

Things that elicit pain or create pleasure can happen at any time during our life and get tucked away in our memory, beneath our conscious awareness.

Many years later, we think we are moving through life doing fine, until something happens to trigger the brain into the same response to avoid a similar pain or suffering. Or to seek a similar pleasure.

When we decide that response is no longer appropriate and wish to change it, unless we resolve the subconscious 'gain' and align the new desired outcome as the 'safe' option, then secondary gains lie in wait to trigger the old reactions.

> There may be instances where the problem is not resolved at the secondary gain level, so we may need to delve even deeper to uncover a tertiary gain.

These are never known at a conscious level which means that the client is totally oblivious to the unconscious layers.

Tertiary gains

Often when we reveal a secondary gain, as the therapist we feel a sense of satisfaction that all will be well now for the client and we move the client forward. Yet sometimes, the challenge is still present for the client. It is always worth checking the unconscious for the potential of multiple layers of unconscious gains. There could be deeper tertiary gains, usually an emotional connection the brain has made much earlier in life when going through a particularly heightened emotional or hormonal growth period. Secondary gains often cause the client to feel relieved, *"Oh, that's why I've been doing that."* When tertiary gains are revealed, it is often a deep and profound epiphany for the client. *"Wow, I would never have known that was there."*

Unless the therapist ensures the client is able to clear these unconscious gains, the client is always at risk of reverting back to those old habits and reactions.

The unconscious part of the mind does not work in logic or intellect – it creates feelings according to its programming. Curiously, this often works against the person rather than for them. This presents as self-sabotage because the unconscious mind responds primarily to its programming.

So, if a client is suffering a condition such as chronic fatigue, it could well be an unconscious need for safety or comfort. The unconscious mind is keeping the person fatigued and tucked away from the world to keep them safe. It may seem like an irrational response but remember,

the unconscious mind does not respond to logic, it responds to programming and ancient survival responses.

For example, when a person wants to quit cigarettes, they have all the conscious reasons why they need to quit, such as health, cost, family etc. All very important and perfectly valid reasons at a conscious level.

So, why would that same person continue to smoke despite the fact that they don't enjoy it, they have health issues, they can't afford it and it's affecting not only them but their family as well?

The fact is that it's an unconscious habit based on an attachment to the secondary gain of helping the person seek safety. (In the case of cigarettes for example, it could be the need for connection, to avoid loneliness, a link to a loved one who used to smoke or still does etc.) The client may logically get the negativity associated with the habit, he or she may even be aware of the logical connection to the loved one or the social aspect, however the subconscious still triggers the urges, cravings and behavior.

Until we update the unconscious programming and disconnect cigarettes as the solution to the need for that connection, comfort, or other secondary or tertiary gain, permanent change is always at risk of not occurring.

The unconscious part of the mind is caring for and protecting the person by meeting an unconscious need for comfort – or whatever the deeper level feeling or need is; it could be a sense of belonging or control or to feel calm or many other things. That need is a feeling that overrides all the intellectual and analytic thoughts of the conscious mind. So, while on a logical level it makes no sense for the person to keep smoking, at an unconscious, feeling level, if smoking is fulfilling a need that cannot currently be fulfilled without smoking, the person will continue to smoke. The same reasoning applies for many other addictions.

Kristine's story

Kristine came to see me for a standard quit smoking session. The session went well, and Kristine left the office feeling great. The next day, she called and said that it didn't take very long at all for the cravings to kick back in. She had started smoking again the same evening. We booked in another session, but she cancelled. Kristine said she didn't feel ready to go ahead with another session, so I left it up to her to contact me when she was. It took several months for Kristine to return. She explained that, although she had never suffered anxiety before, a terrible feeling of panic set in after our previous session which led to a strong urge to smoke again. She was concerned that it was the actual hypnosis that had initiated the panic and was worried it would happen again. I assured her that hypnosis didn't trigger her anxiety and set her mind at ease.

In our session, I used hypnosis to search for unconscious secondary gain, speaking to 'that part' of her that went into a panic. There was obviously some reason she suddenly felt anxious, but neither of us knew what that could be. At the conclusion of the session, Kristine said that nothing had come to her at all. No thoughts. No feelings. The only thing that happened was that a picture of her mother floated through her mind. She stated that this held no relevance for her at all. Her mother had died in childbirth and she had been adopted and raised by wonderfully loving parents and had a very happy life. Her only awareness of her biological mother was one photo of her – it was that photo which had floated through Kristine's mind during our session. It was strange, she said, because she hadn't looked at the photo for years.

I felt certain that this had significant meaning. I asked her what her mother was doing in the photo. Kristine responded, *"She's just smiling. She's sitting on the bonnet of a car in a flowery dress and a pair of high heels, holding a cigarette in her hand and smiling."* Then a look of shock came over Kristine's face. *"I get it!!"* she said. *"Smoking was the only connection I ever had to my biological mother. I know almost nothing about her other than the fact that she was a smoker. That's why I panicked. I was losing the only connection I've ever had to her."*

Kristine went silent for a moment, her eyes looking down, deep in thought. Then she looked up and said, *"That's not a connection. I'm done."* She left my office a non-smoker. Just having that insight come into her awareness was enough to break the connection to cigarettes. In my search for an unconscious secondary gain we discovered a deeper tertiary gain that took Kristine totally by surprise.

When we talk about the unconscious mind, we are referring to *the feeling part of the mind*. And yet where do we feel things? We feel them in the body as sensations and emotions. The intricate mind/body connection means that when we are experiencing an emotion in the unconscious part of the mind, we are experiencing those feelings and sensations in the body.

We have all experienced feelings of fear or worry or nervousness. The thoughts are in the mind, but the feelings are in the wobbly legs, the pounding heart, the sweaty palms, the butterflies in the tummy.

> *The feelings are 100% in the body. Which means that the unconscious mind and the body work together as one.*

It's simply not possible for a client to move to a state of mental, emotional and physical wellbeing if the client has more to gain – at either a conscious or unconscious level – by holding on to their condition than overcoming it.

This is the first consideration we must contemplate if what we are doing doesn't work. Secondary or tertiary gain will definitely keep someone stuck.

Annie's story

Annie was a 60-year-old woman who came to see me because she was suffering severe anxiety. She had always been a strong woman – she was "proud of being the driving force in her family".

She ran a successful accounting practice, employed a strong team and had recently reduced her hours down to three days per week. She believed she had created a healthy balance in her lifestyle. She had never experienced any mental health issues before.

Annie was recently injured in a car accident. Her injuries were relatively minor and resulted in an overnight hospital stay before being discharged to rest for a few days at home. After a week, Annie had had enough 'lying around' and decided to return to work.

When she went to leave the house, she had a panic attack. This was the first time she had ever experienced something like this in her life.

As is often the case with panic attacks, the symptoms were so physically intense that she thought it was a heart attack and her husband called an ambulance. Annie was shocked and annoyed when she was informed that the attack was 'just anxiety'. She accepted the diagnosis with skepticism and a certain level of disdain. But despite her skepticism and annoyance, the situation repeated itself over and over again.

Initially, whenever she attempted to leave the house, she would experience very real physical symptoms. After a very short period of time it escalated and started happening when she attempted to get out of bed. Her doctor prescribed medication, but it only made her feel worse.

When Annie came to see me, she was at her wit's end. The panic attacks had been going on for several weeks by this stage and her appointment with me was the first time she had left the house since they'd started. She had literally forced herself to get out and into the car surrounded by her family, who supported her to the point of almost carrying her every step of the way.

As a hypnotherapist with extensive experience in anxiety and panic attacks, I worked with her to resolve the trauma of the car accident and the anxiety itself. I was shocked and somewhat dismayed that after three sessions there was no improvement in Annie's condition at all. Nothing had changed.

IDENTIFY AND ELIMINATE SECONDARY AND TERTIARY GAINS

After a series of questions and an attempt to delve a bit deeper, I explored the possibility of secondary gain. When Annie realized where I was going with my questions, she became annoyed. *"How can you imply such a thing?"* she questioned. *"I am the strong one in my family. I run my business, I keep the home organized, I look after everyone and everything. Do you really think I want to be like this? I have never had a sick day in my life. I need to get back to work. I need to get on top of things again. This is ridiculous."*

Annie became quite distressed.

I reframed my concerns sufficiently to have her agree to doing a further session to explore the possibility of secondary gain from an unconscious perspective and resolve it.

As soon as the session was over, she opened her eyes and with disbelief in her voice she said, *"You were right. I have always looked after everyone and everything. And now, everyone is looking after me. They are doing everything for me. I haven't had to cook or clean or deal with work. This is the first time in my life that no-one expects anything of me. They just want to care for me. And there's a part of me that has yearned for that. But I want to get back to work. I really do, I've had my break, it's time to get on with life again."*

We did another session, thanking the unconscious mind for taking care of Annie and keeping her safe and cared for and then gave it precise instructions that Annie's needs had changed and that she needed to get back out in the world fully functioning.

A wonderful breakthrough. In one session we went from panic, to anger then to resolving the issue. Annie's panic attacks disappeared that day and have never returned.

Isaac's story

Another client, Isaac, was a 67-year-old man who had been in a wheelchair for almost three years. He could potter around inside the house on a walking frame to do things such as get into bed and go to the bathroom. The medical profession could find no physical cause for his condition.
Isaac was showing no improvement from our sessions, so I analyzed and questioned the potential of secondary gain being at play. I thought I introduced the idea with subtlety and sensitivity but, as with Annie, when I approached the topic, Isaac became annoyed.

"Have you seen my wife?" he retorted. *"She is a beautiful, active woman who loves to go bushwalking and hiking and for walks along the beach. I need to be able to live life with her. We've only been married for five years and I have spent three of those years being incapacitated."* He became more upset as he spoke. *"Do you think I WANT to be this way? Are you seriously suggesting I have something to gain from being like this?"*

I explained (again) that we were not talking about a conscious process, but an unconscious one over which he would have no awareness or control. His conscious desire to achieve results meant he was willing to do whatever it took, so we did a session exploring the deeper emotional need beneath the ailment.

After the session, he shared that he had become aware of the reason for his condition. It was fear. He spoke about his wife and said, *"This is her third marriage. She divorced her first husband, but her second husband became very ill and she could never bring herself to leave while he needed her to care for him. My first wife broke my heart when she left me, and I don't think I could handle that kind of hurt ever again."* This was a real epiphany for Isaac.

Consciously, he had desperately wanted to be well and active. Unconsciously, he needed to feel secure and know that his wife would never leave him. He hadn't realized that his intense need for love and security was literally keeping him paralyzed.

Secondary gain can also be a deliberate strategy

I wish to add here that I have worked with clients who have compensation claims in progress or court cases being heard for PTSD, harassment, traumatic incidences or other workplace issues that relate to severe stress, anxiety and other mental health issues.

Clearly, when you are looking at it from a financial or emotional perspective, it is not in the best interest of the client to get well prior to settlement of their claim. Obviously, there will be those people who just want to recover, but there will also be some who feel that they have too much to lose if they recover prior to their claim being settled.

In this circumstance another conscious secondary gain could be that the client does not want to lose their government or insurance payments and benefits. It would mean that they would face a lot of uncertainty with looking for work, having to find a steady income etc. so it is safer and easier to stay unwell.

As I have demonstrated, secondary and tertiary gains can be conscious, unconscious or both. With each of the above examples, we had to delve down deeper into the layers below conscious awareness to discover what each client needed to know to resolve their issues.

In the next chapter, we will take a deep dive into what to do when you think you've done everything.

Remember to download your free
'What to Do When What You Did Didn't Work' resources
www.therapistshandbook.com/resources

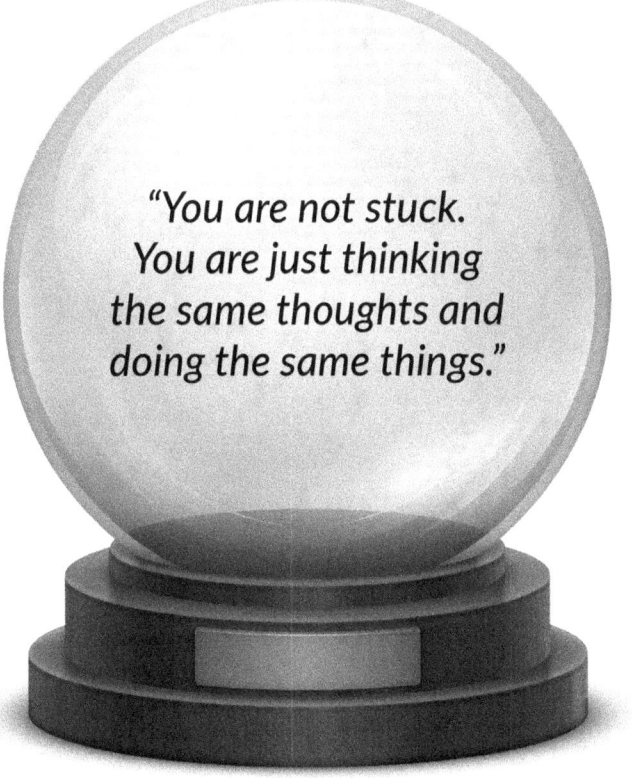

"You are not stuck. You are just thinking the same thoughts and doing the same things."

CHAPTER 6

What Next – When You Think You've Done Absolutely Everything?

"Listen with your ears, your heart, your soul. Then listen to your own inner voice."

John O'Connell

Have you really done everything?

a)   Firstly, look for any obvious omissions or influences.

Your client's surrounding influences and environment are crucially important to their healing.

- ☐ If someone has an anxiety problem and they are living in an abusive environment where they feel unsafe, the anxiety cannot possibly dissipate long term until their living situation is safe.

- ☐ If someone has a drug addiction and the people they spend time with use drugs, it will be extremely difficult for them to stay clean.

This philosophy is true of most situations. We are the sum of the five people we spend most of our time with. You can spend a lot of time helping someone through their mental health issues, but if their environment is not supportive of the outcomes they desire, things will inevitably fail, or any improvements will eventually go backwards.

b) Is the client really ready to change or are they here because someone else wants them to change?

If someone is seeking help because a parent or spouse (or someone else) wants them to change, it's not going to work.

> **Gabby's story**
>
> I worked with Gabby who had been through a pancreas and kidney transplant, so it was vitally important for her to maintain a healthy diet. After a couple of sessions there was really no change in Gabby's motivation to make healthier food choices. We spoke about it and she informed me that she was attending the sessions because her doctor sent her, and her husband insisted on paying for them. She said she'd agreed to the transplant because she believed she would be able to start eating whatever she wanted without having to inject herself with insulin. As it turned out, she was gaining enormous amounts of weight because of the anti-rejection drugs required for transplant recipients, plus she had no energy. The doctors wanted her eating to be more restricted than ever and she simply didn't want to make better food choices. She didn't want to engage in our therapy. She was only there because everyone else wanted her to be. She knew all the reasons why she should want to make the changes, but she just wanted to be left alone.

Our clients must want the change themselves. It must be their choice. They always have the power to choose. No matter what everyone else is choosing for them, the client always makes the final choice. Always be wary if someone else is paying the bill.

c) **Did the client take full responsibility for their own healing and share all the necessary information with you?**

Sometimes, even if you have great rapport and work really well together, there may be important omissions to the information a client shares. This could be for a variety of reasons; perhaps the client feels shame or guilt, perhaps they didn't think certain information was relevant, or maybe some other reason. But perhaps that piece of information is the missing piece to the puzzle. You may need to revisit this with your client to find out together what may have been missed.

d) **Do you, as the therapist need a different approach and some new tools or techniques?**

Learn, improve, diversify and excel. Remember the research showing that therapy was ten times more effective with the best therapists than with the worst therapists? It's important that you become the best version of yourself so that every client can benefit from the best therapy possible.

- ☐ Strengthen your communication skills
- ☐ Refine your craft
- ☐ Expand your knowledge
- ☐ Learn new techniques
- ☐ Find out what works by being curious and creative.
- ☐ Research, broaden your horizons and watch the world open up for you, your clients and your business.

e) **Reflect on everything you do frequently. The wins as well as the challenges provide us with unique learning experiences every time.**

According to the presuppositions of NLP, we have all the resources we need to succeed.

So, if your client hasn't succeeded yet, have you tapped into the right resources? Both yours and your client's.

Who's stuck – the client or the therapist?

The first thing you must do is question and reflect. Be insightful with your observations about yourself, as the therapist, the therapy itself and the engagement of the client. And, of course, the best cure is always prevention. So, if what you did, didn't work, reflect, learn, improve, change and grow so that you become a better therapist for your future clients.

Be curious

Take an honest look at the entire process and reflect on what worked and what didn't. Don't beat yourself up. Have an honest look at yourself and have an honest discussion with your client. Remember, this is not about placing blame, it's about improving your effectiveness as a therapist and tapping into your client's ability to resolve their issues.

Based on research evidence[1], there are certain qualities and actions of an effective therapist that can guide all therapists toward obtaining consistently greater results for their clients.

The most effective therapists have high-level interpersonal and communication skills which include:

* Warmth and acceptance

* Perception

* Empathy and understanding

Their clients feel understood and as a result they trust their therapist and believe they can help them.

As a therapist, it is important to objectively analyze your own interpersonal skills. If the interpersonal therapeutic relationship with your client is well established, you will be able to have an honest, open discussion designed around the fact that you are both keen to keep working toward a successful outcome and are both prepared to work out what has and hasn't worked and where to go from here.

> To do this, you could ask yourself the following questions with regard to your clients:
>
> 1. Did I actively listen to and really understand their feelings, their history, their culture and beliefs, their humanity, their heart and their soul? Or
> 2. Did I listen through therapeutic ears that hear only the presenting issues as my mind categorizes the challenge and searches for the right treatment modality?
> 3. Can I honestly and objectively feel certain that my client felt safe, heard, valued and connected?
> 4. Did I understand and provide for their needs and wants?

---

[1] http://www.scottdmiller.com/wp-content/uploads/2014/06/Supershrinks-Free-Report-1.pdf

There are further questions I'll explore later in this chapter, but I want to address these questions in more detail first.

Clients sometimes feel that therapists are distant and disconnected. Many people seeking therapy are suffering because of beliefs that they are not loved, valued or accepted for who they truly are. Many have a core belief that they are not good enough which can stem from childhood challenges, abuse or neglect. Symptoms may manifest in different ways such as depression, violence, narcissism, anxiety or even physical illness or pain.

The symptoms can be vast, and the reasons can be complicated. They have a real need to feel heard, valued and understood. If they sense that their therapist is 'clinical' or 'distant', they feel disconnected from the therapeutic alignment and will either be resistant to therapy or drop out altogether.

As I write this book, I am experiencing this phenomenon in present time. Just two days ago, I worked with a man named Toby. I saw him for an initial complimentary consultation. Within a few minutes, I knew I'd be able to help Toby and he voiced that he would like to work with me. At the end of our appointment he told me that I was the fifth person he had been to see professionally, and I was the first one he felt comfortable with. He felt as if I was the only therapist who understood him and could help him.

This is an astonishing revelation.

Why is it that so many professionals with training, expertise and good intentions, come across as 'superior, cold, and clinical'?

Since that appointment two days ago, Toby's partner has booked in for a series of sessions and two of his siblings are planning on traveling a significant distance to come and see me. Likewise, just two weeks ago, another client, Anna, contacted me with a similar story. I now also have sessions booked in for both her son and her husband. I note that in both of these cases, the client acted totally on 'feeling'. It wasn't my certificates or qualifications or anything else. It was the way I made them feel during that initial meeting.

My belief is that they should get that same feeling with every therapist. Learning to connect with a client on a feeling level is something that we all need to strive for. You may be the best therapist in the world for this client but unless they 'feel' connected, they will either be resistant or go elsewhere.

Do we sing to their souls?

At the 2017 *Evolution of Psychotherapy* conference in Anaheim, USA, Scott Miller, co-founder of the International Center for Clinical Excellence, talked about research exploring the effectiveness of various forms of psychotherapy, discussing why fewer people are turning to psychotherapy and asked why, statistically, 57 percent of people do not even return after the first session. That's an enormous number, 57 percent!!

He also presented research documenting psychics achieving the same or better results as psychotherapists (psychologists, counselors etc.) and discussed how, annually, more people attend and pay to work with a medium, clairvoyant or psychic than a mental health practitioner.

Why is it that psychics often achieve significantly better results than mental health professionals and physicians? The research showed that psychics simply gave people what they wanted in a way that made sense, was appealing and most importantly, they matched the client's world view, rather than imposing the view that the problem is in your thoughts, behavior, emotions and brain chemistry. He suggested that psychics formed stronger alliances because they were aligned with their client's preferences, background and world view. Scott poses the question to all psychotherapists, *"Could it be because we fail to sing to their souls?"*

This is an interesting perspective not generally talked about in therapeutic circles. If we are to become the best version of ourselves as therapists, we need to be aware of the research and take the findings on board.

> *Scott poses the question to all psychotherapists, "Could it be because we fail to sing to their souls?"*

We need to look critically at our own world view and ask ourselves if we are really doing the best we can with the skills we have and the knowledge available to us. We need to approach every client by combining two different perspectives:

- ☐ What our expertise tells us and
- ☐ What the client actually wants

As mentioned earlier in the chapter, let's continue with the questions we may find useful to ask of ourselves when dealing with clients.

1. **Do I enter each session with a spirit of partnership and collaboration with my client and appreciate that they have their own level of wisdom and strength or, because of my training and expertise, do I consider myself superior to my client in my role as a therapist?**

Every one of us knows how it feels to be in the presence of someone who makes us feel like their equal and with whom we feel connected. Conversely, we all know how we feel when we're with someone who makes us feel inferior and disconnected. If indeed the therapist is the defining factor in the effectiveness of the therapy, we all need to take a closer look at how we relate to our clients – and more importantly – how they relate to us.

2. **Am I aware of the subtle cues I am always conveying through my body language? Am I aware that I am always communicating something – even when I think I'm not actively communicating at all?**

> *Studies have surmised that only seven percent of the meaning of our communication is conveyed through words, 38 percent through tone of voice, and 55 percent through body language.*

Whether these percentages are totally accurate or not has been a topic of some debate. It is, however, undeniably true that our body language and tone of voice are a major factor in the way others interpret our communications.

When we are speaking to another person, it's not our words that are the defining factor in how the other person interprets the communication, it is the way our words make them feel.

The same words spoken with a different tone of voice and use of body language will convey an entirely different message. And when there is a pause – or silence – the non-verbal communication is even stronger. When a client leaves our office, it will not be our words they remember; it will be the way we made them feel and the messages they interpreted from the overall communication. And this is a hugely defining factor in the overall effectiveness of the therapy and the client's ability and willingness to engage.

3. **Are the techniques I am using getting the desired results, or do I need to be more creative and explore different options?**

We only know what we know

Sticking to a defined set of techniques is unnecessarily limiting to the therapist, the client and the effectiveness of the therapy. If you look at almost any progressive industry, people must constantly upgrade their skills and knowledge. Experience alone is not enough. I have worked with colleagues who boast many years of experience. To me, being experienced means that with every passing year you learn more, expand your knowledge, broaden your outlook and develop new skills. It means you are constantly building on your current level of knowledge.

The therapist you are today is different to the therapist you were this time last year. Why? Because every day provides an opportunity to learn and grow. There is a vast difference between someone who has had ten years of experience during which time they've changed and improved and grown – and someone who has had one year's experience repeated ten times over and is still the same limited therapist they were ten years ago.

4. **Am I imparting my own views and values on my client or guiding them to explore and discover their own resources and find their own solutions?**

In my opinion, it is vitally important, as therapists, to keep our own values and beliefs in check.

They are not relevant to our clients, nor should they be. If a therapist, a medical practitioner or anyone else were to instruct you to do something that you believed to be inappropriate for you at this point in time, chances are you would choose to cease therapy rather than go back to someone who was trying to push their own ideas and values onto you. I recently came across this situation.

Alison's story

Alison came to see me for acute anxiety and depression. She had inadvertently put herself in a position where she was alone with a male colleague, whom she thought she knew and trusted, only to find herself in a very compromising situation where she was coerced into a sexual act. Filled with anger, fear and guilt, Alison sought help from a psychologist. He informed her that before he could help her, she must confess to her husband, and she must do it immediately.

Knowing that such a confession would surely destroy her marriage, and believing that her life would be destroyed in the process, Alison did not go back to the psychologist. Even worse, her anxiety increased because she was terrified that the psychologist might contact her husband and tell him what he knew. This, of course, would never happen. No psychologist would betray a client's confidentiality. Still, Alison was not able to think logically, she was stuck in her own fear and angst and as a result felt threatened and extremely anxious.

Our role as a therapist is to help each and every client gain strength, clarity and peace. We are here to form a productive partnership, not give instructions or commands based on our own judgements. In this situation, the psychologist lost a client and Alison gained nothing from her session, in fact, she felt far worse because of it. This was a total lose/lose situation.

Alison is not a bad person, but sometimes bad things happen to good people – and good people do regretful things – but they are still good people.

We will all have our own judgments about whether or not Alison should have confessed what happened to her husband, but it is not our role to impart that judgment. We don't know what her husband is like, what their relationship can withstand or what the outcome will be. Our role is to work with the client and help them to become empowered to make their own decisions from a place of peace, strength and clarity.

> *Our role is to work with the client and help them to become empowered to make their own decisions from a place of peace, strength and clarity.*

It is absolutely crucial during the initial interaction to initiate trust with your client. This will subsequently encourage co-operative engagement in the therapeutic process. This strong bond of trust, established with the client early in therapy, becomes even more firmly embedded over time. The foundations of the therapeutic relationship form a solid, collaborative, purposeful partnership as the goals for therapy are established. When you reflect on your relationship with a challenging client, reflect on this aspect and learn.

5. Have I given my client enough information in a way that they can understand and accept?

When people go to a mental health professional for help, they often want an explanation for their symptoms or problems. They need to feel that the therapist has:

- ☐ the patience to hear and understand the issues they are struggling with
- ☐ the knowledge to be able to give them some sort of an explanation as to what is happening, and
- ☐ the expertise to guide them through the healing process.

When the explanation resonates comfortably with the client's attitudes, beliefs and values, culture, and worldview, the client will feel a high level of compatibility with the therapist. They will feel a connection with the therapist because they can make sense of what they are hearing and feeling. This instils a sense of comfort, safety, trust and certainty. It provides an environment where the client is likely to establish the belief that they can overcome their difficulties. It also creates positive expectations that are fundamental to the success of the therapy. Curiously, an underlying scientific truth of an explanation is unimportant. What matters is that the explanation given by the therapist seems plausible to the client so that engagement and collaboration will be enhanced.

This approach is extremely effective because information is presented to the client in a way that feels right and inspires positive expectations. The client works in partnership with the therapist and takes healthy actions to enable their own healing. You could even go as far as to say; it offers hope where there may previously have been little or none.

Julianne's story

Julianne came to me with premenstrual dysphoric disorder (PMDD). I researched the condition and believed that hypnotherapy could absolutely help her.

She had been to many doctors over the years and apart from explanations about hormonal imbalances that were unable to be corrected by medication (with no explanation as to why her hormones were imbalanced) she had no understanding of her condition and no-one offered any hope of a cure. I shared with her my version of an explanation for her symptoms.

I hypothesized that years and years of holding in all the anger and sadness from her childhood and other life experiences, and pushing down all the hurt, fear and other negative emotions, had caused all that negative energy to manifest in this issue. I feel certain that there would be little or no underlying scientific proof of that explanation. It did, however, resonate beautifully with Julianne's beliefs and values. She said that for the first time ever, she felt as if someone finally understood what she was going through.

After just two sessions she was completely asymptomatic, feeling healthier than she had in years, looked 15 years younger and was ecstatic with the results. The lesson being, if you haven't resonated with your client's view of the world, do it now.

> *It's never too late to become a little more insightful and creative. It's never too late to become more empathetic and open.*

6. Have I objectively monitored my client's progress and been willing to be flexible?

It's important to monitor every client's progress in an authentic way and be flexible when it comes to recognizing and responding to their changing needs. If the client is not genuinely experiencing significant improvements, or if resistance is apparent, listen, understand, adjust your style and find a different approach. Otherwise you risk losing the client or providing therapy that is ineffective. It's never too late to become a little more insightful and creative. It's never too late to become more empathetic and open.

Verbal and nonverbal cues

As therapists, we must be aware of the verbal and nonverbal cues that indicate the client may be resistant to either the therapist or the approach being used. This must be followed by a willingness to dig deeper, learn new techniques, be guided by the client and accept that it's OK to admit to the client – and yourself – that there is no failure here, just feedback which is vital to accept and learn from.

Modifications might involve subtle differences in the manner in which the therapy is delivered, use of a different therapeutic approach, referral to another therapist, or use of adjunctive services such as naturopathy, acupuncture, etc.

A highly effective therapist has a firm belief that together the therapist and client will work successfully. This is not a 'pie in the sky' type of belief. It's a sound credence based on knowledge and experience. It is a conviction based on feeling comfortable enough to delve into the more difficult aspects of the communications, address the core problems and be creative and open to new techniques and solutions with an attitude of optimism and certainty.

The essential point here is that the most effective therapists consistently achieve progress with his or her clients because they are continually improving and enhancing their own skills and knowledge.

Helen's story

Helen was a vibrant woman in her late thirties who came to see me for severe anxiety. She had previously been to a counselor followed by several visits to a psychologist. She told me that the counselor was a lovely woman, but after a few visits she could see that nothing was improving. Helen had lost all confidence in the ability of the counselor to help her resolve her anxiety.

She then sought help from her doctor who prescribed anti-anxiety medication and referred her to a psychologist. Helen believed that the medication made her feel worse and her sessions with the psychologist were also ineffective. I saw Helen for four sessions. Her anxiety in general terms improved significantly. One of her main issues, however, was her inability to drive her car due to severe panic attacks. I did all the usual questioning and reflecting. I also searched for secondary gain. (Perhaps, on some level, Helen felt comfort in having to be driven around by her husband.)

Unconscious secondary gain must be the answer I thought, but there simply appeared to be no secondary gain at play here. There was no history of a car accident or other trauma that could account for Helen's driving related panic attacks. Helen could clearly remember the last time she felt calm and happy while driving. It was a very pleasant memory from over a year ago when she went out with friends for an enjoyable afternoon tea. It was quite a distance from her home and she happily did the forty-minute drive to the venue and back home again.

To the best of her recollection, Helen had a panic attack the very next time she tried to drive and has continued to have them ever since. But nothing, it seemed, happened to account for this reaction.

What was I missing?

No trauma! No secondary gain! Helen had even tried different processes such as EFT (Emotional Freedom Technique, also known as tapping) and she had seen a naturopath.

I tried some different approaches including Time Line Therapy and Rewind technique. Our therapeutic relationship was strong. Rapport was excellent. Helen told me that she truly believed that I would be the one to help her resolve this issue and she clearly wanted us to keep working together. I wasn't going to give up on her, but the way forward wasn't clear.

What was I missing?

I discussed Helen's case with a colleague and decided to try a new regression technique to search out the underlying cause. We had already done some regression work without success, but this was a new approach for me, one I hadn't used before. With the knowledge and belief that, on some level, Helen had the resources and answers within her to resolve this dilemma, we went ahead and tried a different hypnotic technique.

Following the session, Helen told me that she kept seeing images of the scar on her upper arm and getting visions of the horrified looks on the faces of two of her 'friends' who subsequently smirked at Helen's misfortune. I hadn't previously been aware of any scar.

A year or so ago, Helen went to her doctor about a lump she had on her upper arm. The lump was a benign fatty tissue deposit. Helen had the lump surgically removed but her GP removed too much skin and couldn't adequately sew the wound together. This left Helen with a deep, wide scar.

As we explored this new insight, it became evident that Helen did suffer a trauma that day (the last time she drove calmly) at the afternoon tea. She confided in me that she had never worn a sleeveless dress since that day and she suddenly remembered that the next time she got in her car, she was going to be seeing those two 'friends' again and her panic manifested because of them – not because of the driving. She had felt deeply hurt and humiliated by their reaction. It was as if they were pleased that she had been disfigured in this way.

Since then, Helen had distanced herself from that group of so-called friends and her inability to drive had given her the perfect excuse. So, on some level, there was a traumatic experience, and, on some level, a secondary gain was in play. I didn't know this and neither did Helen.

We both just had to be willing to delve deeper and uncover enough layers to find it.

The story has a happy ending. Helen saw a plastic surgeon and although it's not completely gone, the scar on her upper arm has been cosmetically improved. We did some more work together and Helen is driving again and has not suffered any further anxiety or panic attacks.

What if a client wants you to fail?

Finally, there is another possible scenario altogether as to why therapy isn't working for a client. Perhaps the client simply cannot be helped or refuses to be helped. One of my teachers and mentors, Tad James, once told me the story of a client who came to him for help.

The client boasted that he had already seen many therapists in the areas of psychology, counseling, hypnotherapy, NLP and more. He had spent several thousands of dollars and been treated by 'the best of the best'. No-one could fix him. He then challenged Tad, *"You're supposed to be one of the greatest. Let's see what you can do?"*

Tad believed that this client was, for want of a better word, proud of the fact that no-one could 'fix' him and wore it like a badge of honor. He believed that while the client held this belief, and was determined to see it through to fruition, it would remain true for the client. Tad would be added to a long list of failures of this man's belief system. Tad simply told him, *"I can't help you,"* and left it at that.

The late Milton Erickson, known as 'the father of modern hypnotherapy', told Rob McNeilly, *"It's a fact that some people are not going to get over their problem. I think that a lot of therapists have this idea that if they do the right thing, everyone can be cured. And in that context, it's arrogance. We can't cure anyone. All we can do is help them to see more possibilities."*

If the client feels some need to hold onto their issue, wants to test or challenge the therapist and subsequently give them a 'fail,' it can never be a win, win situation. In other words, if the client is firmly holding onto the belief that the therapist must fail to validate the client's belief system, there can never be a true alignment of goals.

If this occurs, there can only be two possible outcomes. Either the client must make the shift to wanting to become well rather than needing to hold onto their current belief … or … the therapist must accept that they will not be able to help this client, in which case it may be best not to work with them at all at this time. Enabling the client to hold onto their belief by allowing them to experience another failure would be counter-productive for the client and the therapist. It has to be a judgement call though.

If the therapist can assist the client to understand what they may be consciously or unconsciously doing by 'daring the therapist to fail', and how it is only hurting themselves by keeping them stuck in their issue, it could present an enormous breakthrough opportunity for the client. It could indeed simply be a secondary or tertiary gain to uncover.

To summarize, reflect on and analyze your effectiveness in the following areas;

a) Is the client's environment conducive to and supportive of the changes they seek?

b) Do I exude warmth and acceptance, perception, empathy and understanding?

c) Am I listening with my heart rather than just through therapeutic ears?

d) Does my client feel safe, heard, valued and connected?

e) Have I ensured my client's total commitment and preparedness to fulfill their role in their own healing?

f) Am I certain that my client is in therapy because they want help, not because someone else wants them to get help?

g) Am I communicating clearly, effectively, professionally and compassionately?

h) Have I created a spirit of partnership and collaboration?

i) Have I defined clear goals for the therapy based on my client's desires, wants and needs?

j) Am I providing information in a way my client can understand and accept?

k) Am I using strategies that my client resonates with and awakens their own resourcefulness?

l) Am I checking in with my client for genuine feedback on their progress?

m) Am I being creative and exploring new insights and options?

n) Do I actively learn and utilize new and different strategies and techniques?

o) Do I enjoy being fully present and thinking outside the box?

Once you have openly and honestly reflected on all of these aspects, you have the foundations from which to create new levels of empathy, expertise, creativity and success.

You can download free
'*What to Do When What You Did Didn't Work*' resources here: www.therapistshandbook.com/resources

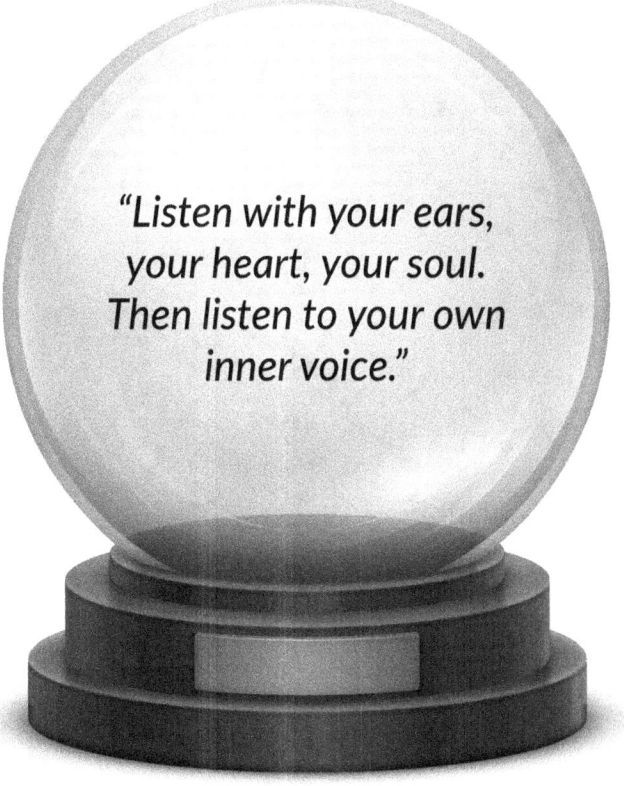

"Listen with your ears, your heart, your soul. Then listen to your own inner voice."

CHAPTER 7

Pull Out the Big Guns –
Expert Tips from Global Leaders

> *"Today you can do what you did yesterday, and tomorrow you can do what you did today, or you can build onto that which is already excellent."*
>
> John O'Connell

I am thrilled to be able to bring expert tips from some of my colleagues; international leaders in our field who have generously shared their top tips to overcoming resistance and challenging clients. Thank you Shelley Stockwell-Nicholas, Brian Perry, Rob McNeilly, Sheila Granger and Freddy Jacquin for generously sharing their expertise.

Freddy Jacquin

Freddy Jacquin is the founder of the UK Hypnotherapy Training College and Jacquin Hypnosis Academy, author of the book Hypnotherapy and has helped over 30,000 clients in private practice and group sessions. His techniques have been used by therapists all around the world.

Trust

The main ingredient in any personal communication is trust. In a hypnotherapy or any therapeutic situation, trust is even more necessary.

When a client meets a hypnotherapist for the first time for therapy, they may have many misconceptions about hypnosis. One of these misconceptions is the belief that they will be asleep and not know what is happening or what they are doing, another is that the hypnotherapist will have control of their mind. If the client is not reassured that this is not the case and exactly what hypnosis is, they are very likely not going to accept any suggestions given to them and therefore not overcome their problem. So, trust is paramount in hypnotherapy.

Also, trust that you are a good person and want the best for your client. Remember that your intent and expectation is paramount; your expectation that the client has all the inner resources, strengths and ability and understanding to overcome the problem they want freedom from, and your intention that the client will achieve that freedom.

Rapport

There is a lot written and said about the importance of 'rapport' in a therapeutic encounter and many hours are spent studying how to build rapport. I believe that rapport is there to be lost, not gained. The easiest way to lose rapport is to try and gain it, because when you are consciously trying to build rapport with someone you are not acting naturally, the equivalent of trying to be nice.

I believe that rapport is there to be lost, not gained.

I would suggest that you know how to communicate because you have been communicating from the moment you were born, so just be yourself.

I teach my students to run this verbal loop in their mind when working with a client, *"I care about you and I want you to be well."* If you feel it's appropriate you can say it, but you should always hold that thought in your heart.

Pretalk

Pretalk is a strange term that we assume means pre the hypnosis part of the session. The truth is that the hypnosis should start the moment your client enters the therapy room. Everything that you say and do, should be aimed at the client's outcome. Attitude, confidence, certainty, expectation and belief, are as important as the words that you say in the 'pretalk'.

If the client is concerned about being hypnotized or being in trance, explain to them that they are already in trance, albeit an, 'I can't stop doing what I am doing' trance. Then demonstrate some eye-open hypnotic phenomena to prove what you are talking about. Explain to the client that they will be aware, all of the time, but that everything else, other than your voice and the reason they are there, will be peripheral.

I generally say this to my clients, *"You can listen to me if you want, but I don't mean this rudely, I'm not interested in your conscious mind. You have tried to overcome this problem consciously and it hasn't worked. This is an unconscious process and your unconscious mind will hear and understand everything that I may say and take from it what is needed for you to free yourself forever."* This gives even the most concerned client the confidence to allow you to help them.

One of my favorite quotes is from Milton Erickson, and I believe fundamental to success for the newbie hypnotherapist. Erickson was working with a cancer client who was dying and in terrible pain, which Erickson relieved the patient from. Someone asked Erickson if he knew that he could do that (relieve the pain). Erickson said, *"I had my doubts, but what I had no doubt about *was that I could keep my doubts to myself."* This is sometimes harder to master than the hypnotic techniques and protocols, but I believe is of utmost importance in the hypnotic encounter.

When it doesn't work

When using hypnosis for therapeutic reasons the results can be, and often are, close to miraculous. We, as the therapist, want to help our clients to resolve their problem, that is why we do this work. When it doesn't happen, we question ourselves as to what we did wrong or what we could or should have done differently. These questions are good for us to ask because they help us grow and improve.

We have in our tool bag lots of brilliant tools, but sometimes no matter what we do we just can't seem to help our client. This is the time to remind ourselves that we are human not Gods, and that we are dealing with human beings not machinery, and sometimes no matter what we do, we cannot help that client.

Challenging clients

We often hear of a client who is resisting therapy or reluctant to change. I personally had a client who actually said to me, *"This will be a challenge."*

I told him that if this was going to be a challenge, then I would definitely lose, because I was there to help him not to challenge him. I believe that all therapeutic encounters should be a collaboration, with everyone involved working toward the same outcome.

The question I ask all my clients is, *"Do you want to change?"* If a client is in your therapy room because someone other than the client wants them to change, tell your client to go away and come back when they truly want to change, because if you don't you will be wasting your time and taking their money under false pretenses.

All power to you and all those whose lives you will change for the better with your love, skill and understanding.

Shelley Stockwell-Nicholas

Shelley Stockwell-Nicholas is co-founder and president of the International Hypnosis Federation and the author of many books and educational DVDs and CDs. She has trained thousands of students around the world.

The power of language

A lot of hypnotherapists, psychologists and psychiatrists don't pay enough attention to their language. The words you speak have great power. When a person walks in the door they're already hypnotized and every word that comes from your sweet lips is hypnotizing them for a positive or negative outcome. If you say to them, *"How can I help you today?"* that's more positive than asking, *"What's your problem?"*

If you were to say to them at the start, *"If you were to leave this session today having achieved what you came for, what would that be like for you?"* you already have them establishing the result they want before they even begin.

Active listening and giving back the client's exact words and phrases, and only addressing concerns if they ask via their dominant senses, is important. Your best pretalk is to let them know, *"I can help you."*

When clients are resistant

Sometimes there is a delayed reaction and your client will get the result they're after a little later. Sometimes they need a follow-up session and always the therapist must ask themselves, *"Did I key into their dominant senses, requests, style and frame of reference?"*

> *A hypnotherapist is a paid mirror-holder. The person who is coming to you knows more about themselves than their mother will ever know, their family will ever know, or their therapist will ever know.*

A big mistake that therapists make is not checking in with the client and instead making up a story in their heads about what the client needs.

Poor therapists believe that they know the answer to another person's issue, and they do not. A hypnotherapist is a paid mirror-holder. The person who is coming to you knows more about themselves than their mother will ever know, their family will ever know, or their therapist will ever know.

There's only one person who knows them well, and that's themselves. The most important thing you can do for a client is to have them tell you what needs to happen, during the pretalk and also from the trance state. As a really good hypnotist or a good therapist the most important thing you can do is to have your client go in to find out what they need for themselves.

People are not in fact 'resistant'; rapport first is essential and results come when you key into the client and get over yourself.

> *Of all the process I've come up with I think joy is the solution; laughter is what we're all after.*

When you key into your client, you use their frame of reference and then link the solution to the information that they give you from their higher self, dominant senses, what they do for fun, their desired outcome and their sense of success. Processes naturally evolve from there. Of all the processes I've come up with I think joy is the solution; laughter is what we're all after.

The biggest mistakes

One of the gigantic mistakes hypnotherapists make is they assume that in order to solve the client's problem, whatever it is, they need to go to the source of the problem, dig out all the crap from the past and shovel through it to find out the answer. That is a huge mistake because they are not God.

The best thing to do is conduct an interview first and then put the client in a trance, whether through self- hypnosis or inducing trance. From the trance state conduct the interview all over again, talking to the client's higher self, their all-knowing wise self, that knows the truth for them. A question you can ask that higher self is, *"Is it in this person's best interest to go to the source of this problem to solve the issue, or is it to just solve the issue?"*

That way you empower the person, who's wise beyond wise, to give you the truth of what needs to happen next.

The two biggest errors that we can make are not paying attention to our language and not entrusting the person with their own solution. Both of them can be harmful.

I take the position there's no such thing as a resistant client there are only resistant therapists.

Rob McNeilly

Rob McNeilly is a clinical hypnotherapist and trainer who studied with Milton Erickson. He founded the Centre for Effective Therapy in 1988 to introduce Ericksonian Hypnosis and the Solution Oriented Approach to hypnosis, counseling and coaching in Australia.

Resistant clients

I take the position there's no such thing as a resistant client there are only resistant therapists. So-called difficult clients are just doing what they're doing. We call them difficult when they're not doing what we think they should be doing.

The best way to deal with resistant or difficult clients is to prevent that. Prevention is the best term of cure always. We can prevent difficulties and prevent resistance by some very simple steps as therapists.

Listen

Often therapists have an idea of what is required, and they have a protocol. That way they don't need to listen to what the client wants and that's where a lot of the difficulties and resistance comes from.

First of all, we need to listen to what the client's concerns are. Who is this person? What do they want? And in particular we need to listen to what their expectations are.

If we ask the client, *"What do you want from this session?"* some people will say,

- *"I want to understand why I've got this problem."* Some people say,
- *"I want to know how to handle it better."* Others will say,
- *"I want to get rid of it."*

People have different desires, different worries, and different reactions to what's going on.

At the second visit, if the client says there's no improvement and the therapy has made no difference, I've found that the best thing is to go back to the start, back to the basics. Ask them again, *"What is it that you want from this therapy?"*

If I listen, I realize that their answer is what they said last time, but I didn't listen to them. I have my own wisdom and my own expertise, so I think, *"Oh I know what really needs to happen here,"* and I head off on my own tangent.

We can listen from our intellect for information so we can diagnose the pathology that's going on, or we can listen from our heart, from our soul, and from our experience.

Traditionally therapists listen for pathology so they can treat it in a medical model. The medical model works beautifully for medical conditions, but it turns out that the human suffering that brings people to therapy does not fit in with the medical model.

Milton Erickson put it so beautifully when he said, *"Therapy is being sought not primarily because of the unchangeable past, but because of some discontent in the present and a desire to be better in the future."*

People want to feel better, so we listen for what is it that *they* think would be helpful for them to get better and have a better life.

How people learn

When we listen to our clients, we discover how they learn and how they resolve issues. Some people learn by listening. Some people will learn by repetition; they just have to do this over and over again and eventually they learn. Some people learn by doing nothing and then suddenly a light goes on, and they get it just like that.

We can use metaphor; tell a story. Take a plant for example. You find out what that plant needs and then suddenly that plant starts to grow. And when it grows then it might have fruit or flowers. There are stories about possibilities and those stories are a part of the human experience. We often learn through stories.

What's missing versus what's wrong

In our training we tend to listen for what's wrong with our clients and then we apply some theory, some technique or some approach to fix it. But what we really need to do is listen for what's missing. If we listen to what's missing for our clients, we can help them to reconnect with that or to learn it.

Listening for what's missing is diametrically opposed to listening for what's wrong. If we find out what's wrong with someone that needs fixing, we're going to get some resistance.

Someone's got a sore throat. I'll give them penicillin, but some throat infections are viral and they're not going be affected by penicillin. Other infections are going to be resistant to penicillin.

If we just have one thing that we use, we are going to find that it doesn't always work and it's going to create resistance. But if we ask, *"What's missing from this person?"* and start to listen to this person's own experiences, then we are much more likely to find what works for them. It's going to happen more respectfully, more quickly, and more permanently because it comes from within the client, not from outside.

Listening for what's missing is diametrically opposed to listening for what's wrong.

When we find out what someone wants, what's missing for them, what their needs are, what they like, and how they learn, we've got a winning combination. We are asking, *"What works for you?"* And by doing that we engage this person in their experience through what they are already doing. When we discover what they have that already works for them they're not going to be difficult or resistant.

Some therapists aren't willing to listen to the client. They're looking for a strategy or a specific technique. If we stick to a specific protocol, we're going to be ineffective.

Validation

Sometimes people need validation. If they're suffering and can see no way out just having someone validate their feelings can make a huge difference. Legitimizing someone's suffering, when it is done sincerely, can really help to ground them. When we say to a client, *"You've been through hell. You've had a terrible lot to cope with. You've been suffering through this for a long time,"* this validates their feelings and makes them feel understood.

In summary, difficult clients and resistant clients are best dealt with by preventing that situation from happening, and by refusing to think of someone as difficult or resistant. Instead look at what additional perspective, approach, idea or possibility we can offer.

If none of that works, validate.

Also, my invitation to you is to start to see that a lot of people are more resourceful than they realize. All of us are, actually. And all have resources that we're not used to utilizing, yet it's possible for us to do that. Not guaranteed but possible. If we as therapists can hold that possibility, sometimes the client will expand into that possibility.

Bryan Perry

Bryan Perry, hypnotherapist, psychologist, trainer and author, has had a long and distinguished career in Australia and internationally since the 1950's. He founded the Hypnotic Research Association, the South Australian Association of Hypnotherapists and the Human Resource Centre.

Take a different approach

If what you are doing isn't working, then you have to look for what you've missed or consider unconscious secondary gain. And then, of course, you need to do something different. There is no point in repeating the same type of thing you've already done over again, unless you want the same results, because if you repeat the same process, the brain will continue to process it in the same way.

You need a different approach. A technique that causes the brain to process information in a different way will get a different result.

Over the years I have learnt, developed and used a wide array of strategies to elicit a different response from the brain. I've used a technique where I have the client go through a series of physical movements with their limbs – increasing the speed faster and faster – exhausting the body and mind to the extent of lowering their defenses and then quickly I'd ask them a question about what they are holding back, and they would tell me. It takes just a few minutes and can be extremely powerful in retrieving critical information from the unconscious mind. This process breaks through resistance which the client didn't even realize was there.

It is essential to learn, refine and use techniques which will allow us to implant the seeds of positive change as we gain an understanding of the psychodynamics of each patient and his or her problems. We must also weed out negative concepts embedded in the subconscious minds of clients over time.

Dreams

One of the most powerful techniques I've used is that of hypnotically induced dreams. This is a relatively simple diagnostic procedure which works extremely well in 40 to 50% of cases where other more superficial techniques have failed.

Dreaming is a natural part of the activities of the mind.

The purpose of dreaming has been conjectured over the centuries by people ranging from ancient theologians and great philosophers, to more recent psychoanalysts such as Freud, Jung and many others. The interpretation of dreams has been debated within varying schools of thought and there are many ways of categorizing and analyzing dreams.

In 1956 I was involved in a three-year experimental research study group on hypnotic phenomena and dreams. We found that individual subjects, while in hypnosis, could identify and make sense of their own dream symbols and use this to facilitate their own healing process without outside interpretive contamination. We used this process to have patients uncover their own deepest issues and to resolve them.

This, and other techniques, were powerful tools to help patients overcome their own difficulties and get a great result.

Roles

Ideally all therapists will have a plethora of qualities to draw on as there are many roles they must play as they work with their patients. There are also certain negative qualities that must be vigorously excluded. The extent to which the therapist adopts or sheds these tendencies will determine their success rates achieved with their patients.

When I say there are certain roles we must play, these include the following:

- ☐ Detective – correctly perceive underlying messages revealed in the initial interview and subsequent sessions.
- ☐ Counselor – listening and easing the patients suffering by applying appropriate words and meanings.
- ☐ Sage – being able to process information effectively and wisely.

- ☐ Friend – being open and approachable so as to enable trust and rapport.
- ☐ Saint – being understanding, patient and supportive.
- ☐ Prophet – being able to reasonably assess the results of any form of intervention before you even begin to use it.

The negative characteristics to be shed are:

- ☐ Judge – we must never sit in judgement of our patients.
- ☐ Policeman – we must never make our patients feel guilty.
- ☐ Messiah – it's imperative to avoid self-aggrandizement or the belief that you are somehow doing the work. The patient is doing the work. As a therapist, you are merely the facilitator.

> *it's imperative to avoid self-aggrandizement or the belief that you are somehow doing the work. The patient is doing the work. As a therapist, you are merely the facilitator.*

Sheila Granger

Sheila Granger is an internationally renowned professional clinical hypnotherapist, trainer and author. Her much sought-after expertise in the field of personal and professional transformation has changed thousands of lives for the better.

Who's the hypnotist in the room?

When I think of clients where the result hasn't been there or it hasn't gone the way I thought it would, I always remember a phrase that was said to me early on in my career; there can only be one hypnotist in the room.

As the hypnotherapist, you are there to take the lead. You're there to have an influence on your client's behavior, so it's important to take on that role and have them follow your lead.

You need to be very mindful there is only one hypnotist in the room at any one point of time; and make sure it's you.

When I have a client, who is resistant or challenging, I analyze the situation and what I usually discover is that I allowed them to become the hypnotist in the room. We need to be wary of that. We are the one controlling the direction of the therapy, not the other way around.

If a client comes for weight loss, for example, we have to ask, what has this person actually come for?

Even though there may be underlying issues that we have to deal with somewhere along the line, they've come for that one thing; they've come to lose weight and in their mind that's what they want to do.

If you have a client who comes for one thing, but then starts sending you in different directions by saying they have depression or start bringing up other issues, you need to be very clear about what you are working on and what direction the therapy is taking. If we allow the client to take us in all sorts of other directions, we are not actually working on what they came for in the first place.

If we allow them to become the hypnotist in the room, they don't get the outcome that they originally came for. You need to be very mindful there is only one hypnotist in the room at any one point of time; and make sure it's you.

Motivation

People must be motivated if they are going to change. We need to keep our clients keen and on board. It's not a process where somebody can just come and sit, and we are going to do something to them. We want an active process and to keep that happening we need to create some kind of 'quick win'.

If, after the first session, our clients go away and they immediately notice some kind of change, they are going to be more willing to look at the other areas because we've created that quick win.

If we don't create that quick win in the first session, everything can start to go downhill from there. Because if that doesn't work, the client may feel discouraged. Also, we may question whether the next thing will work. And then the energy changes.

Sometimes, because people want *everything* to change, they don't really notice that *something* has changed. We need to highlight the things that have changed so we can build on those.

Intentions and beliefs

When you do a session with a client, what are your beliefs?

You must believe in your own mind that you are expecting this to work. Because a lot of the time things can come from our own self-doubt. It never helps anyone if you are thinking, *"Oh, I'll keep my fingers crossed that this is going to bring about results,"* or, *"I'll pray that this works."* You must genuinely believe that the client can achieve their outcome. A quick win will help in this regard.

Sometimes, because people want everything to change, they don't really notice that something has changed.

Another thing I always do before a session is tell the client that we don't talk about it afterwards. The reason is because it can make the session less effective if everything comes to conscious awareness, so it's best just left alone.

Following the session, I might simply ask what they are doing today to flip their mind onto something else. It creates a bit of amnesia and distraction. Then I'll add, *"I did say that I didn't want to talk about the session, but I have to say, you were absolutely brilliant. There weren't any problems at all. Everything went well. I'll see you next week."* This is a great way to finish the session on a good energy.

Environment

There are so many things that come into play with how we stage the sessions; our intention, our belief, our confidence and even things like environment make a big difference as well.

I started off working from home. I changed the spare bedroom into a therapy room and then eventually I moved into private rooms. When I moved into a private room, I got more equipment, including a system of headsets mikes and a GSR meter. I wore a headset and so did my client, and I put a GSR meter on the client's fingers, so it was a very professional setup. Many clients commented that it was a completely different experience to when they'd seen a therapist before.

In reality, it probably made absolutely no difference than when I was working from home, but it provided a different experience for the client.

Resistant or challenging clients

As a hypnotherapist, a lot of the time what we call resistant or challenging clients probably were not resistant or challenging when they first sought out help. They are seeking you out as a last resort. They've been everywhere else, and so far, nothing has worked.

Unfortunately, we are rarely the first point of call. When they've been through the system and everything else has failed, they think they're a failure, nothing's going to work. They can come in as a resistant person. Sometimes that resistance will get in the way of the treatment.

I offer complimentary consultations for the client's benefit, but also for mine as well. I want to know, *"Is this person workable, have I got rapport with them or not. Can I help this person?"*

I think that sometimes we have to pick and choose who we work with. And at that point we need to find a way to filter out the people who don't want to change. When we first train and we have this amazing set of skills, we think, *"This is amazing. There are so many people I can help with this."* We want to help everyone, but sometimes we want the change more than the client does.

Clearly on some level, there are people who are looking to fail again, as though they have something to prove. We've got to realize that we can't fix everything. We can't fix everybody. If I feel that I haven't got rapport and they're not very workable (and in the past I've even worked with people who try to make me feel uncomfortable) looking back I have to ask, *"Who was the hypnotist in the room?"*

There can only be one hypnotist in the room – so make sure it's you!

Maggie Wilde – The Potentialist

Maggie Wilde is a 10-time award winning author, a clinical therapist and publisher to the therapeutic and coaching industry. She is widely known as the 'Coaches' Coach' and is the creator of 'Control, Program, Rewire (CPR) Brain Training Model' and the S.C.A.L.E Healthcare Business Model.

The right questions and the partnership

I believe there are no *'difficult or resistant'* clients, simply clients with programming challenges or a solution you haven't come across yet. It doesn't mean you can't meet that challenge and guide your client through to their solution; you simply haven't asked the right question of the client's conscious or subconscious processes to access the key that will unlock the solution.

For me, the success of any treatment plan, will be determined by the level of commitment that I have made toward outlining and obtaining acceptance of the 'partnership agreement' at the outset. If I have clearly outlined the importance of the client's role in their treatment, and I then proceed to perform my role effectively, which is to actively listen to the breadcrumbs my client leaves me, and respond appropriately by asking the right questions, at the right time, I open the doorway for the client to reveal their solution and get through any resistance. *(Breadcrumbs are everything the client says and doesn't say; all they do and don't do throughout the course of their treatment.)*

When I am willing to be compassionate to my client and their perceived challenge, but lead the room, and we've both embraced that partnership, we become a 'team' that is working toward the same desired outcome.

Curiosity… getting out of your own way

Curiosity for me is the greatest tool I can use in my work with clients and practitioners. I am constantly curious about the next step.

If there is resistance to the next step, rather than blame myself for not knowing how to help, or the client for being 'resistant', I am curious to know what I and they don't know yet. Curiosity leads me to ask more questions, and when I ask more questions and get out of my own way (deleting the persistent tail-end voice that wants perfection and wants it today), then my own energy frees up to allow the client's energy to flow more freely too.

Adapt and keep learning

Equally important when dealing with, as yet unsolved challenges, is the ability to adapt, duck and dive with a well-stocked toolbelt of strategies to draw upon. To keep learning and adding skills, listening to what's 'not' said, and developing new or adapted strategies when they pop into your mind. Never say never to new ideas. When we are truly working from that space that opens doorways to solutions, we will adapt even well-worn strategies to meet the clients' needs anyway.

For example, I might do a particular technique one way for years, but suddenly I just 'know' that when I 'tweak' it slightly for this particular client, they will respond differently. Then voila, the resistance disappears, and we move on.

When we work from a place of flow, when we are truly connected and attuned to the client, listening to even what's *not* being said, then a voice greater than us, often pops into our head to guide us and the client to a deeper resource of clues and solutions too.

As the therapist, we get out of our own way, when we step out of the 'therapists' ego that wants to be the one who 'fixes' this. When we step into a resource greater than us, greater than the client and greater than the problem, we dissolve mountains of 'resistance effortlessly.' The unconscious processes that heal from the inside out know all the answers to all the questions you and the client have ever asked, and the questions you and they don't know to ask yet. When you allow those processes to flow, the solutions reveal themselves.

Tertiary gains

When clearing resistance, I actively switch my curiosity on again. I am not satisfied when the subconscious reveals a secondary gain, I continue asking for clarity and confirmation that there are no sneaky tertiary gains lurking beneath a deeper layer.

Often a therapist will be satisfied (perhaps even relieved), when a secondary gain reveals itself, content to think that the 'client must be free of this resistance now.'

Be aware there may be further gains, in multiple layers lurking that may be triggered by something else. So, get curious and ask more.

Whose belief is that anyway?

I also have a phrase on repeat in my mind when resistance appears. I will remind myself to ask, *"Whose belief is that anyway? The client's, someone else's or mine?"* If my instinct says it's my belief or judgment, doubt or fear getting in the way of treatment, I actively remind myself, *"This is none of my business, I am simply the channel to guide this person to their solution."* If it's the client's or someone else's, I revert to curiosity and start connecting, asking more questions and 'listening' more.

"Build onto that which is already excellent."

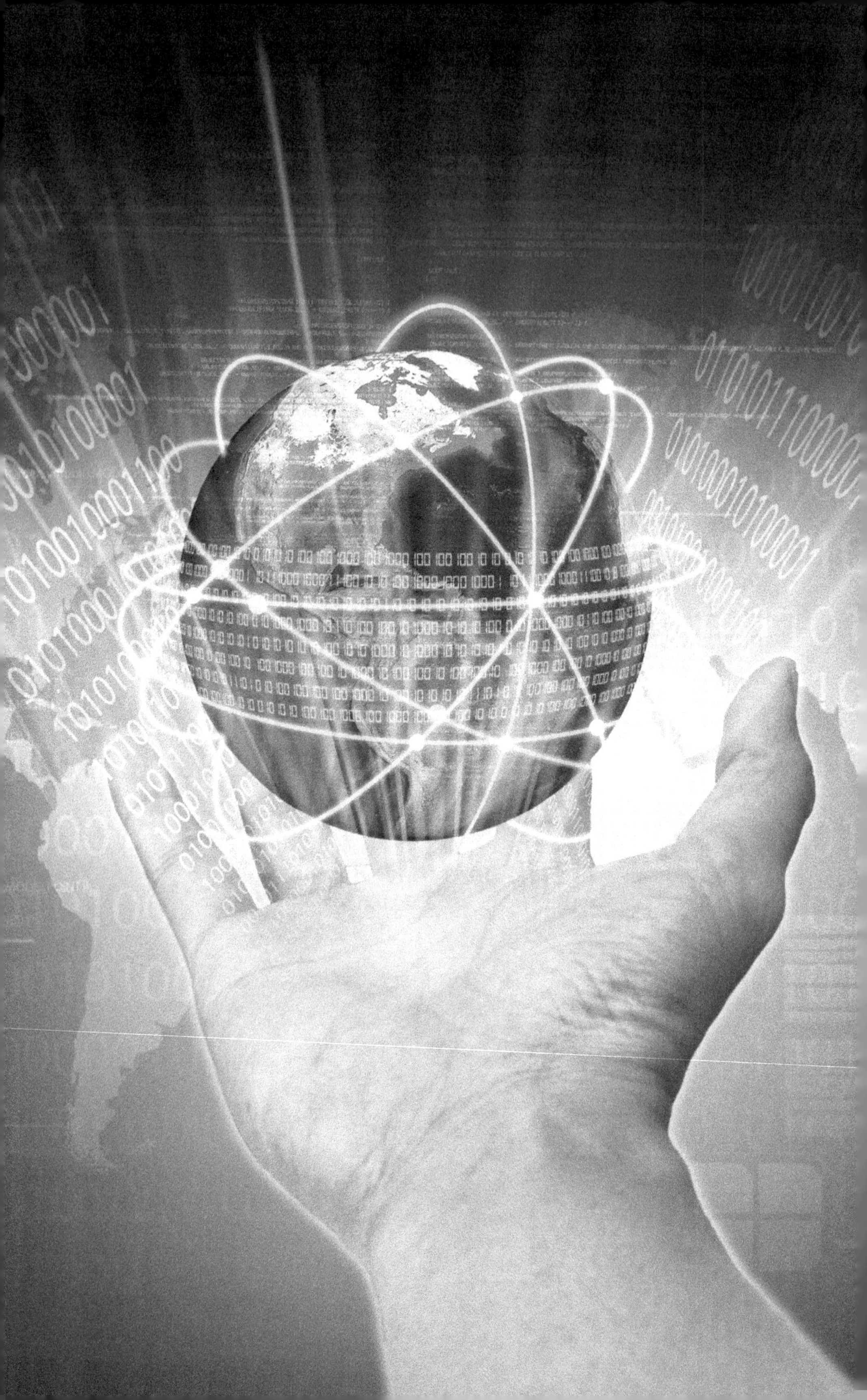

CHAPTER 8

How to Expand your Practice to Work Online

"All you need is a vision and a great internet connection."
Leonie O'Connell

In this ever-changing world it's important to be flexible and to find other ways of working with those changes. Moving work practices online has become necessary in recent times, but even so, expanding your practice to a global clientele makes good business sense.

As we've discovered in the previous chapters, therapists need to create an environment of trust from the first moments of interaction with their client. During the initial contact, clients are sensitive to verbal and non-verbal cues from the therapist and can sense their level of acceptance, understanding, and expertise. An environment of warmth and capability is necessary throughout the entire therapy program. You might think the kind of environment needed for therapy might be harder to create online, but that's not necessarily the case. There are things to consider though, which we'll go into in this chapter.

Working with clients online has many similarities to working with them face to face, with regard to what you say and do, how you present yourself and how you run your actual session. However, there are some extra skills required in dealing with the technology. If you are great with technology, there will be some good tips and information in this section. If you are terrified of technology, I'll provide some simple solutions that will have you doing online sessions using equipment you already have.

1. Invest in a good internet plan

First and foremost, if you are going to do online sessions, make sure you have excellent internet connectivity. This may mean upgrading your internet plan to a greater capacity and faster speed. It may mean doing your sessions from a different location e.g. your office instead of your home. It will also mean ensuring that your client has good connectivity as well. I have worked with many clients who have better connectivity in different parts of their house and have had to locate themselves in a certain room. It may be better to be on a computer rather than a portable device so that you can plug into the modem rather than relying on WiFi. The last thing you want happening is constant drop outs.

Interestingly, the program you use can make a difference. Be prepared to make changes and adjustments if needed. I recently worked with an overseas client who was located in a rural area. We started out using Skype, but the video kept freezing. We then tried Zoom and the sound was echoing and delayed. We attempted FaceTime with slightly better success. Finally, my client suggested Messenger video and it worked. I wouldn't have considered this option and I don't really understand all the technological nuances or why this would occur, but the session went well, and we maintained a good video and audio connection. I have also had situations where the video and audio just didn't sync perfectly with Zoom so we continued to use the computer video while using our phones for the audio; we could see each other on the computer but we were speaking through our phones.

2. Be prepared

Have all your equipment, music, notes and scripts, client resources, PowerPoint presentations and anything else you will need, prepared and ready to go. If you are using a program such as Skype or Zoom, you can learn how to pre-load all of these resources into the program, share your screen, add the music etc.

> *Finally, check that your insurance covers online sessions, especially if you are working with overseas clients.*

If you take the time to learn how to use these programs, it will assist you to run your sessions smoothly with everything right there at your fingertips. You will move through the various functions of the program as you move through the session. But if you come across a situation (as I mentioned earlier) where you have to switch strategies, be prepared for that. Have a Plan B. Have all of your resources ready and at hand. Finally, check that your insurance covers online sessions, especially if you are working with overseas clients.

3. Prepare your client ahead of the appointment

Prior to the session, send any necessary forms via email so they can have them completed and returned prior to the appointment. Send your client written instructions outlining what they must do to prepare. This is very important. Waiting for the unprepared client to prepare themselves or working with an unprepared client can be disruptive and very time consuming. I learnt this a long time ago in a few separate situations.

Tom's story
In the first situation, I had finished the pretalk discussions and asked my client, Tom, to get ready for the session. Tom assured me that he would be undisturbed in his bedroom for the duration of the session and that his family, who were in another part of the house, knew not to interrupt him during this time. Tom was connected with me through his phone. I asked him to put it in a position where I could see his face. He placed the phone on a pillow on his stomach. I suggested that he find a better place for the phone as I was concerned that having it on his tummy might not be a very stable position. He assured me that this would work perfectly for him and we went ahead with the session.

Here's what happened. As Tom started to relax into the session, he shifted his position and the phone fell over. Tom repositioned the phone and assured me this wouldn't happen again. It happened three more times. One of those times it fell right off because Tom jolted, and the phone landed on the floor. When Tom got up to get the phone, he had to also go to the bathroom. But that's not all. At one point, Tom's cat, who was in the room with him, decided to jump up on the bed and snuggle in with him. So, the cat was moving around and purring and because the cat was near the speaker of the phone, the purring sound was amplifying through my speakers and back again to Tom.

Other examples

Another client I worked with had a bird flying around in the room. It decided to peck at the phone and totally disrupt the session. On another occasion, it took my client over 15 minutes (following the pretalk while I was waiting on my end of the video call) to set herself up in a comfortable position, try several ways to set up her phone so I could see her (coffee table, chair, using books to balance it, adjusting and re-adjusting), get her cat out of the room, give the dog a feed so that it wouldn't start barking and then go to the bathroom and get a drink of water.

Lesson learned the hard way. I now send a full checklist of what the client needs to do, well before our appointment begins, to be fully prepared for the session and I recommend you do too.

4. Be professional

When you are doing online sessions, you could be running them from somewhere as casual as your bedroom or hotel room or somewhere more formal, like your office. Always remember, you are working in a professional capacity and you must present yourself as such. Be dressed and present yourself as you would if you were working face to face with a client in your practice. Be aware of the background image in your video. Start the video before the session begins and see what your client will be seeing. You do not want your client to be seeing an unmade bed in the background or have them staring into bad lighting. Use what you have available in the space to provide a comfortable, simple, well-lit image and background. Make sure the lighting is favorable and there are no visually distracting aspects to the video.

Try different positions in the room. The space may not be perfect but do the best you can with what you have.

Ensure privacy and confidentiality

If you are working from home, make sure the space is private. Once, during a first appointment, I had a client ask me to visually show her around the room I was working in because she thought she heard a voice and wanted to be assured that there was no-one else within earshot. As usual, I was working from the spare room in my home which is set up as a small home office room. As always, I had the door closed ensuring privacy for myself and my client. I was more than happy to scan the whole room for her so that she could see the environment I was working from and knew that she was in a private, safe space.

So, on that note, you never really know exactly what may happen during a session or what your client might need to see or hear in order to feel safe and comfortable. Have your setting, your personal presentation and your space conducive to the therapy.

If you are using a program like Zoom, you can add in a virtual background, but these can sometimes look fake and provide a different type of distraction. Remember, you are creating a space for therapy here. Just as if you were in your office or clinic, you want the space to feel safe, comfortable, private and professional. Keep it simple and pleasant.

5. You can start with minimal equipment

With the right equipment and technology you can run an extremely professional set up right from your own living room. But when you are starting out doing online sessions, don't get too caught up in the equipment side of things. If it is all too daunting it may prevent you from getting started at all. Just get going with the basics and work your way up.

Remember, the most important aspect of working with clients – whether face to face or online – is you. If you have a smart phone, a tablet or a computer, you have enough equipment to get started. If you are working with limited equipment, you will simply need to be prepared.

- ☐ Send the client any forms, diagrams or other visual information via email well before the session.
- ☐ Have your notes and scripts printed and easily accessible.
- ☐ Have your music ready. In my first online sessions I had a CD playing on a CD player for the background music. It worked fine. I simply tested the sound by asking the client if the volume of the music and my voice sounded right from their end, made the adjustments and started the session.
- ☐ You can use headphones with a microphone to ensure clarity of sound and minimal background noise. If you are using a smartphone or a tablet, purchase a tripod to stabilize it. A portable Luvo Beauty Ring Light for Smart Phones is great for providing a soft, natural lighting effect.

Most of all, the equipment is only secondary to the relationship you build with your client and the quality of care you provide. You are the defining factor here – not the equipment. Be prepared, be confident and be yourself.

6. Software and equipment advanced options

There are several software options for running online sessions. Some of the more popular programs would be, Skype, Zoom and Go to Meeting. There are free versions and paid upgrades for most programs. You can learn how to use the features in these programs such as being able to screen-share, upload music, virtual whiteboard etc. through their own online learning tutorials or through instructional videos on YouTube. You can access free trials and decide what works for you. When it comes to technology, you literally have a world of information readily available at your fingertips through your computer keyboard or your touch-pad.

Most of all, the equipment is only secondary to the relationship you build with your client and the quality of care you provide.

For a more professional, streamlined, advanced online setup, here is a list of equipment suggestions.

a) Webcam

At the time of writing this book a quality webcam such as the Logitech HD Pro Stream C922, will give a far better-quality video than most built-in webcams on laptops or other devices. The advantages of a good quality webcam are that it interacts quickly to the feed, will have a built-in stereo mic, a full HD glass lens and work with a wide range of software options. It will bring a high quality to your video feed. It will also have the capacity for using a green screen. A green screen may not be a consideration right now but possibly, as you expand your online practice, you may move into video advertising and marketing. At the time of writing this book, the average price for a quality webcam will be under $200 or less than 100 pounds sterling.

b) Microphone

A good quality microphone will bring high resolution sound and another level of excellence to your video sessions. One example at the time of writing this book is the Rode NT USB which can be purchased online or from a good electronic store for less than $200.00 or 100 pounds sterling

c) Headset

A good headset which is comfortable to wear and gives clarity in sound will create great immersion in the sessions. There are many options available. The Rig 600 LX is a gaming headset with two different types of microphone, LX1amp and Dolby, and will exceed your requirements for less than $130.00 or 70-pounds sterling.

d) Studio Lights

Good studio lights offer an even light and a better-quality video. There are times when I might look tired, but with some make-up and the right lighting I look fresher and alert. Some studio light kits come complete with curtain backdrop and green screen. An online search will bring up several good options well under $200.00 or 100 pounds sterling.

e) Drawing Tablet

A drawing tablet makes it easier if you are using a program with a virtual white board. A whiteboard makes it possible to draw diagrams and displays for your client online. While this is a great feature, using a virtual whiteboard with a mouse is difficult. The tablet makes it much easier. At the time of writing this book, the Ugee M708 10 x 6 inch is a good option. It will cost around $60.00 or less than 30 pounds sterling. Search online for 'Drawing tablet for virtual whiteboard.'

Taking our work online will only increase in the future. Many therapists have already embraced online sessions because it provides unlimited potential for reach and growth. You can work with anyone, anywhere, anytime providing you have a reliable internet connection. It provides an opportunity to help people you would normally not be able to reach. In times of crisis, it provides an avenue to connect with and serve the people who need you most. It's easy, convenient and cost effective. It can fit in with your lifestyle and the lifestyle of your clients. Time and distance are no longer an obstacle.

"All you need is a vision and a great internet connection."

WHAT YOUR FUTURE HOLDS

Keep learning to become the best version of yourself.

"The best way to predict the future is to create it."
Abraham Lincoln

Working in the field of therapy, whether it be psychology, counseling, hypnotherapy, life coaching, NLP or any other modality, can be the most rewarding profession possible. It can also be a difficult and perplexing profession with many ups and downs.

When our clients achieve phenomenally successful outcomes, it's a wonderful feeling for all involved. The ripple effect can spread far and wide. It's not just the client that benefits, the positive effects will ripple out to their children and families, their friends, their relatives, their employer or employees, their work colleagues and perhaps even people they just pass by in the street. And the same ripple effect applies for the therapist. Everyone feels good. Everyone wins. So, it is not only our desire but our overt responsibility to do our best work always and achieve the greatest results possible.

Being a great therapist encompasses many aspects. We know through observation and research that the many facets of being a successful therapist must be present and balanced if we are to achieve consistently great outcomes for our clients.

Having a wonderfully caring manner and the ability to connect with someone, build trust and develop genuine rapport is a vital starting point. It will, however, only take you and your client so far, unless you have the knowledge and skills to apply techniques and strategies which will shift your client from where they are to where they want to be.

By the same token, having a strong set of strategies and techniques will only take you so far if you lack creativity, flexibility and the ability to recognize what is and isn't working.

Subsequently, creativity and flexibility will only take you so far unless you have new ideas and insights to draw on and utilize.

Techniques simply provide a defined procedure or a standardized approach that may or may not be effective when you are working with something as mysterious and complex as the human mind. There is no denying techniques are important. They provide a process that has been developed by someone with expertise, experience and influence. The danger is that sometimes we can get so caught up in standardized techniques that we lose the ability to flow with and allow for the changing direction of the therapy. The rigidity and structure of a standardized technique can be very restrictive.

However, lessons from the greats who have come before us and techniques developed by people who are knowledgeable in their field provide great learnings on which to base our approach. The secret is to take the expertise of others, use it, play with it, build on it and blend it with your own unique style, creativity and expertise. You can then combine that with information gained from the aligned partnership with your client and create something meaningful and wonderful.

In 1675, Sir Isaac Newton famously penned the quote, "If I have seen further, it is by standing upon the shoulders of giants."

You will only gain new ideas and insights if you embrace every opportunity to learn and change and bring passion and commitment to everything you do.

Forty years ago, Both John and I were nurses working in a public hospital on Sydney's northern beaches. Over the years we have worked in the childcare industry, the hospitality industry and for the last ten years, we have run our own successful hypnotherapy practice and founded the Academy of Therapeutic Hypnosis.

Every change has presented a huge learning curve, and the learning never ends. This career, hypnotherapy, has presented the greatest learning curve of all. The more you know, the more you realize there is to learn. Our understanding of the human mind and the human condition is still in its infancy and evolving every day. It is by far the most fascinating area of science yet to be fully explored. And our personal journey in the exploration of the workings of the mind has taken us all around the world.

We have trained with experts from around the globe. We have worked with clients, both personally and online, from all corners of this planet and we have travelled to amazing destinations because our business has provided us with the work/life balance that no other profession has provided us in the past. I have delivered hypnotherapy sessions

- on a cruise ship in Alaska
- a resort in Bali, and
- a motel room in New York.

And we never plan to stop learning. One thing we have discovered is that nothing very exciting ever happens within your comfort zone. But when you step out of your comfort zone, it is not uncomfortable at all after a short while. Your comfort zone continually grows and expands right along with you. And it's wonderful.

Our own ongoing learning and development, along with our work with clients, greatly benefits our students because we bring the essence of everything we learn into everything we teach.

It is our sincere belief that hypnotherapy transforms lives like no other form of therapy can. We believe that every doctor, psychologist, counselor, life coach or therapist of any kind will improve their results by learning to enhance their current modality with hypnotherapy. I even know physiotherapists who achieve far greater results with chronic pain sufferers by incorporating hypnotherapy strategies into their treatments. Imagine going to a dentist who could eliminate someone's anxiety simply by using hypnotic language throughout the procedure.

Imagine teaching a parent a few simple techniques to enhance their child's self-esteem and confidence in their everyday life.

The possibilities are endless when you work with the deeper levels of the human mind.

The Academy of Therapeutic Hypnosis runs a range of courses from beginner to advanced and specialized topics such as medical hypnosis, quit smoking, weight loss and more. Whether you are wishing to start out in a new career or want specialist training around a particular issue, we have many training options available – in person or online.

If you would like to contact us personally for any of our training or mentoring programs, we would love to hear from you at info@aoth.com.au

APPENDIX

The Structure of a Great Pretalk

1. Set the scene

It is vitally important to realize that your client is making judgements about you from the first moment they lay eyes on you. They will take a mental note of the way you greet them, your general manner, the way you dress, the way you speak to them and many other things. They may not even be consciously aware they are doing this. We all do this whether we realize it or not. But the only important aspect of this multi-layered analysis is the way you make them feel.

- ☐ Do you make them feel welcome, safe, comfortable and in good hands?
- ☐ Do you make them feel like you have the caring nature and expertise to be able to help them?
- ☐ Do they feel like you are someone they can trust and confide in?

As therapists, from that very first moment, we need to connect with the client in a natural way with respect, care, professionalism, and friendliness. This first meeting sets the scene for the entire feel of the therapy. It is a determining point as to whether or not the client will even return for another appointment.

2. Ask the right questions and be very specific

Clients are often very good at telling their story and defining exactly what they *don't* want to feel any more. They are often clear on what they don't want but very vague about what they do want. They will say things like, "*I don't want to feel sad and anxious all the time. My mind never stops. I can't think straight. I just want to feel better."* But if you ask them what they mean by "better" they often can't answer that. They will say things like "not anxious" or "normal" but still can't define what normal means.

I always make a list of what the client wants so that we can literally tick it off by the end of the therapy sessions.

If someone can't even state how they 'want to feel' it is probably because they can't conceive of the idea of what it would feel like if they were free of the anxiety or whatever issue they want to resolve.

As therapists, we can make assumptions that we believe would be the desired outcome for the client, but they are only assumptions. Always ask and get a clear answer to, "How do you want to feel instead?" Only then will you, and the client, know if you are progressing in the right direction.

I always make a list of what the client wants so that we can literally tick it off by the end of the therapy sessions. This is important for two reasons.

- A. Firstly, you need to know that what you are doing is working.
- B. Secondly, if the client is getting great results and feeling much better, they can sometimes forget how bad they were feeling when they initially came to see you and they do not even realize how much progress they have made. It's very rewarding for the client and the therapist to actually have a written measure of the improvements.

3. Explain how you work, the process you will use and the client's role

Create a partnership right from the beginning. The client must be an equal and fully engaged partner in this process. They are not there to have this therapy done to them. They are an equal and active participant. Explain the process.

- ☐ Define your role as the therapist.
- ☐ Define the client's role in their own healing process.
- ☐ Ensure the client understand that you are only 50% of the equation here – they are the other 50% (perhaps more).

4. Know what part of the mind you are working with and proceed accordingly

Many therapies work with the logical, thinking part of the mind. This part of the mind works in words and thoughts and it is what we refer to as the 'conscious' part of the mind. If this is the case, engagement, practice, repetition and ongoing commitment is imperative. The client must understand that this is an ongoing process that requires them to take responsibility for the work that needs to be done to achieve their desired outcome.

Hypnotherapy works with the deeper, feeling part of the mind. The part of the mind that we refer to as the unconscious or subconscious. The client needs to understand that the language of this part of the mind is feelings and images. They need to be ready and willing to follow all instructions and engage in a process of active imagination. Because we are working with the unconscious part of the mind, it is a quicker process that assists the client to make changes at a deeper, feeling level.

5. Understand where your client is, and what they need in the short term to achieve their long-term goals

If your client is highly anxious, depressed or angry, they are most likely stuck at some level of the fight, flight, freeze response.

- ☐ Being stuck in the fight response translates to unwarranted anger (the body wants to fight and is pumping adrenaline.)
- ☐ Being stuck in the flight response translates to unwarranted anxiety (the body wants to run and is pumping adrenaline.)
- ☐ Being stuck in the freeze response translates to a state of depression where the client just wants to hide away, often not even wanting to get out of bed. Just feeling stuck - frozen!

These feelings originate in the deeper feeling part of the mind that does not respond to logic. It's like the mind and the body are on 'emergency alert' and they cannot think clearly or logically. The client often knows there is no logic to how they are feeling but they can't move past it.

The quickest and most effective way to get the client out of these feelings that are keeping them stuck exactly where they are – feeling angry, scared, distrustful and stuck – is with hypnosis.

6. In summary

- ☐ Connect by being genuine and caring
- ☐ Ask the right questions
- ☐ Get very specific
- ☐ Develop an equal and committed partnership with the client
- ☐ Understand exactly where they are at emotionally, and
- ☐ Work with the part of the mind that is required to be able to make a difference in the short term so that they can get the desired results in the long term

To download free resources from the book go to
www.therapistshandbook.com

BONUS CONTENT

A 12-step guide to setting up your own successful therapy practice

When you're starting out in your own business there are several aspects to consider.

    A. Firstly, there is the physical aspect of setting yourself up to work with clients.

    B. Secondly, there is the emotional aspect. Starting your own practice, becoming your own boss, helping people on your own terms, and structuring a business to work within your lifestyle can be both exhilarating and daunting.

Emotional attachment is a wonderful thing when you are creating something new. Be passionate about everything you are doing and totally committed to what you are creating.

Emotional detachment is an important skill when you are working on the business aspect of setting up your own practice. Get good advice with regards to the financial and legal structure of your business.

Be passionate. Be practical. Be prepared.

Generally speaking, professional advice about setting up your own practice would include doing prep work such as creating business plans, doing market research etc. While this is good advice, I have found that people who are in the therapy and caring professions are not always strongly business minded and the thought of doing these types of things cause them to never even get started. It all becomes too overwhelming. But it need not be. Here is my step by step advice covering the mental, emotional and professional aspects of starting your own practice. And remember, with every step you take, things start to flow, and it all becomes easier as you go. Action creates momentum.

Get your mental and emotional attitude right.

Value yourself and your work. Commit to doing whatever it takes and trust yourself to succeed. Be great at what you do. Get very clear on what you are good at and define, in your own mind, the type of client you want to attract.

Ultimately, doing great work and making a meaningful difference to someone's life will be your most important marketing strategy – word of mouth. People will travel huge distances and pay good money based on a great recommendation from a happy client. People also share extraordinary amounts of information via social media, so you will probably never even be aware of what information is being shared about you.

Make sure that you always have your mental attitude, emotional commitment and professional expertise perfectly balanced so that there are many happy clients out there sharing great information about their experience with you. Commit to what you are doing, work within the areas you feel competent and confident.

Be prepared to ride any 'ups and downs' as you get started. Stick to the basics. Keep things simple. Do excellent work. Always over deliver.

Do market research.

Market research is an important aspect of setting up your practice, but don't get too caught up in it. Know your area. The keys to focus on are:

- ☐ If you are setting up in your local area, then you already know the general demographic. If you are starting out in an entirely new locality, you will need to do your homework.
    - o What is the area like?
    - o Is it a tight-knit community that takes a long time to accept new people or ideas?
    - o What is the socio-economic status of the area?
    - o Are there many businesses similar to yours? Who is the competition?
    - o Do you want to be priced in the existing market? Or set yourself apart somehow? You won't know the right answers to these questions unless you do the market research.

These are the types of questions you need to consider. And always dig a little deeper to get a real feel for the area, the people and the potential to run a successful practice.

Choose a niche so that you have a focus for your marketing.

Do *not* try to market everything to everyone. Do *not* try to market yourself. Let people know how you can help them. Your marketing should focus on how you can help the person you seek to attract as your client.

When I started out, I advertised to two groups of people – those who wanted to quit smoking and those who wanted to lose weight. These were areas where I felt both confident and competent. I attracted very specific clients by knowing what their pain points were and offering them a solution. When they experienced success, my confidence and expertise grew. Then through word of mouth, my practice quickly grew.

Through ongoing study and learning, my expertise and client base expanded into other areas. Choosing a niche will not limit you. It will give you the opportunity to choose what you are great at and decide who you work with. As a result, you will do excellent work, achieve excellent results, expand your confidence, generate great word of mouth referrals and create a successful practice from which to expand what you offer and branch into new areas. Everyone wins.

My favorite scenario. Win, win, win, win.

- ☐ Win for your client
- ☐ Win for you
- ☐ Win for the community
- ☐ Win for the planet

Know your legislative requirements.

When you are starting out, you need to make a few decisions about your business entity. For example you need to decide whether you will trade as:

- ☐ a company
- ☐ sole trader, or
- ☐ partnership etc.
- ☐ you need to register your business name
- ☐ organize insurances, and
- ☐ set up your taxation structure
- ☐ You must be aware of any legal obligations and legislative requirements. These are all relatively simple steps that are not as officious as they sound, but they need to be addressed correctly right from the outset. Get all of the groundwork done by researching requirements specific to your state and country of residence so that your structure is solid.

Find a location.

Some therapists set up a home office, while others prefer a room in a professional space. I know many therapists who have been successful with both and there are pluses and minuses to both. The important aspects to consider are safety, comfort, privacy and professionalism.

It's imperative that both you and your client feel safe and comfortable in the environment – on both a physical and emotional level. For example, if you run a practice from home and there are difficult stairs, cracked pathways etc. to navigate, it is neither safe nor professional. If a client feels that the location is isolated, they may feel uneasy, especially during the beginning stages when they have not yet established a relationship with you.

Likewise, a therapist may feel uncomfortable practicing at home with a client who is agitated or behaving irrationally.

Security and safety are imperative for both the client and the therapist. Alternatively, if you run your practice from a professional space that feels too clinical or impersonal, or there is a lot of background noise, the space could be uncomfortable or distracting. If the cost of renting a space is restrictive you could consider sharing a space with another type of therapist. Is the location easily accessible by public transport? Is there parking available? All of these things are to be considered.

Designing your space.

Once you have chosen your location, you can design your space. Choose furnishings and colors conducive to the ambience you want to create – safe, comfortable, private and professional.

Then you need to consider the practical aspects.

- ☐ You will need a system to ensure your client's confidentiality and privacy. A locked filing system for forms and notes and storage space for your business supplies, documents etc.
- ☐ Access to drinking water and a bathroom are also important.
- ☐ Add some personal touches to the room and some soft furnishings. You want your space to be inviting so clients feel relaxed and comfortable.
- ☐ You also need to feel relaxed and comfortable. This is your space. It should reflect the type of person you are, merged with the image you want to present. The ambience you create will affect the way both you and your client feel within this space.

☐ You don't need to spend large amounts of money decorating. You don't need to be extravagant. Just be authentic. Create a pleasant ambience that reflects the type of practitioner you are and the type of clients you wish to attract… and keep it simple.

Financial considerations and business plan.

There are costs to starting out in business. Rent, registrations, insurances, room lease, technology, furnishings, marketing, printing etc. There are many ways to keep costs to a minimum, but realistically you need to have enough working capital to support yourself financially while you establish the business and start seeing paying clients.

If you are seeking finance to start your business, you will very likely need to provide a detailed business plan for the financier. You may need some professional assistance with this. If you are financing this venture yourself, you won't require a heavily detailed business plan, but it is good business sense to have a basic structure or strategy for what you wish to work toward. Consider:

☐ What are your personal and financial goals?

☐ How much money do you need to make each week/month/year to cover the costs of running a practice and to make a decent living?

☐ Specifically, spend time to clarify the income level that is required to initially cover the costs of running your business and then, provide you with the lifestyle you seek.

☐ Consider your pricing and then work out how many clients you would require each week/month/year to be able to achieve that level of income?

☐ How much do you need to put aside for taxation obligations?

- ☐ What marketing budget do you require?
- ☐ Do you eventually want to employ staff such as an office administrator?

Know your fundamental financial requirements and structure your personal and business goals into a written plan so that you can assess your progress as you go. Be crystal clear on your vision. Check in with your progress at regular intervals (don't just do the initial business plan and then forget it's in the filing cabinet. It's a working document and should be assessed at regular intervals throughout the year to ensure you are either on track or, if not, you will know to adjust your actions and strategy along the way.)

Billing.

We are moving more and more toward a cashless society. If you want clients to pay by cash, you will need to make this clear. Other ways to accept payments are via direct transfer (where the client transfers money directly to your bank account) or through a payment system such as Square, Stripe or Paypal so that you can accept credit card payments.

There are many payment collection options available for small business that are easy to set up, convenient to use and have low administration costs.

Decide on your pricing – Respect your worth.

Value your own expertise, set your prices at a level that adequately reflects your value and always over-deliver.

People within the caring professions often have a block when it comes to asking for money. Money is simply a form of energy exchange. Your ability to run a successful business relies 100% on your ability to create a great income. And then everyone benefits.

Your clients pay well and get great value for a fabulous service. They benefit. You get well paid for doing a wonderful job helping people. You benefit. Actually, everyone benefits.

If you cannot afford to run your practice, the consequence is that your business will close down. And that helps no-one. So, recognize if you have blocks with money, do the work to get over blocks about asking for money or understanding and accepting the value of your skills and time to others. You are not asking for anything. You are facilitating a fair exchange that is highly beneficial for everyone. It is a win-win.

Paperwork – Have documented policies and pre-prepared client forms.

Be clear with yourself and your clients about your policies and procedures.

1. When you design your client intake forms, outline any relevant policy points and include them in the consent section of the forms. This doesn't need to be complicated, but you do need to have clarity around pricing, payment options, structures such as upfront payments, payment plans etc.

2. You need to have a clear cancellation policy and refund policy.

3. Procedures around client privacy, storage of documents, reporting obligations and informed consent are also necessary.

4. Document all policies and discuss any of the relevant procedures with your client so that there is a clear understanding. This creates mutual trust and exhibits professionalism.

5. Once again, keep it simple. Don't go into unnecessary, complex details. Create clarity, not confusion.

Network.

Put yourself out there.

1. Introduce yourself to others who may refer clients to you such as doctors, naturopaths and other therapists who compliment what you are doing.

2. Have your information out there where people will see it – brochures, business cards etc.

3. Write articles for newspapers and magazines tackling a relevant topic or offering a solution to a problem.

4. Do talks at libraries, community centers etc.

5. Join networking groups or start a Meetup group.

6. Run corporate events on topics relevant to the audience.

7. Make use of online forums. Never do this with the intention of making money. Ask yourself, *"How can I serve these people?"*

8. Stay true to your purpose to help and serve others.

9. Always be genuine in your communication.

10. Connect with others in an authentic way. If you are giving a talk or writing an article, make sure you share information and ideas that are relevant, valuable and interesting. Make it about them, not you.

Final words of advice.

When you are starting out, never fall for the trap of believing that your clinical competence alone will create a successful practice. Ultimately it will, as your reputation and your standing within the community grows, but not at the start. Realize that it's OK to make mistakes. A mistake is not a failure, it presents a learning curve. You are now well and truly partaking in the 'University of Life'. Every day presents an opportunity to learn and grow and become better at what you do.

Recognize that just because your schooling is finished, it doesn't in any way mean that your education is complete. Keep studying, learning, reflecting and improving on everything you do. Education is a lifelong pursuit. Developing your skills and knowledge while gaining experience, reflecting honestly on yourself and your practice, and expanding your expertise will be hugely important in the overall quality of the service you provide and the success of your practice.

Recognize that just because your schooling is finished, it doesn't in any way mean that your education is complete.

MEET THE CONTRIBUTORS

We are grateful to our expert colleagues from around the world who have contributed to this book.

Rob McNeilly

Dr. Robert McNeilly started out as a medical practitioner in Melbourne. He studied hypnotherapy with the legendary Milton H Erickson and was inspired to create his neo-Ericksonian approach based on respect and client dignity.

Rob founded the Centre for Effective Therapy in Tasmania in 1988 to introduce Ericksonian Hypnosis and the Solution Oriented Approach to hypnosis, counseling and coaching in Australia.

He teaches the Advanced Certification in Hypnosis, building on an Ericksonian Approach and runs many online training courses. Rob is an international speaker and author. He has run workshops in many countries around the world.

Rob was inspired by Milton Erickson's human approach to therapy and created his own interpretation to assist clients. He is known for his graceful ability to approach complex issues and assist clients in a respectful, dignified manner.

Sheila Granger

Sheila Granger is a lifestyle engineer and professional UK clinical hypnotherapist based in Hull, in the north of England. She is internationally recognized for her pioneering work and is known around the world for her work with the Virtual Gastric Band weight loss program.

Sheila is a trainer, speaker and author who runs courses for hypnotherapists, both online and in person, all around the world.

Sheila has been tireless in her commitment to promote the benefits of hypnotherapy and assist hypnotherapists around the globe to enhance awareness of their craft. She also teaches business and marketing skills for hypnotherapists to build successful private practices.

Bryan Perry

Bryan Perry, hypnotherapist, psychologist, speaker, trainer and author, has been practicing as a hypnotherapist since 1952 and has served more than 50,000 patients. He founded the Hypnotic Research Association in 1954, followed by South Australian Association of Hypnotherapists and the Human Resource Centre.

Bryan was renowned for his ground-breaking results with asthma, having eliminated his own severe asthma attacks through self-hypnosis.

At the request of many appreciative professionals who benefited from his work, Bryan began to teach others his valuable skills in 1979. Bryan collaborates with psychologists, psychiatrists, social workers, educators and scientists across Australia and the world.

Bryan was born in 1930, and still now, in 2020, Bryan teaches and lectures in Australia and overseas.

Dr. Shelley Stockwell-Nicholas

Shelley Stockwell-Nicholas, hypnotherapist for more than 30 years, trainer, speaker, media personality and author of over 15 books, is co-founder and president of the International Hypnosis Federation. She has trained thousands of students around the world.

Shelley specializes in effortless mind mastery and hypnosis methods for enlightenment, success, love, money, sports, childbirth, happiness and wellness.

Dr. Shelley has appeared on more than 600 radio and television shows including ABC, BBC, CBS, Good Morning Australia with Bert Newton, and David Letterman. Her own television series, The Shelley Show, won an Angel Award of Excellence for outstanding cable television. From the Los Angeles Times, to the London Daily News, Dr. Shelley is known as a premier hypnosis expert.

Freddy Jacquin

Freddy Jacquin is the Founder of the UK Hypnotherapy Training College and author of the book *Hypnotherapy: Methods, Techniques and Philosophies of Freddy Jacquin*.

Freddy initially studied hypnotherapy out of fascination and interest. He ended up becoming a full-time hypnotherapist due to his desire to help people rapidly change their lives for the better.

Freddy has helped over 30,000 people change their lives using hypnotherapy. He is known for inventing several unique techniques and has been teaching hypnotherapy students around the world for more than 25 years.

Maggie Wilde – The Potentialist

Maggie Wilde is a 10-time award winning author, publisher and online course developer. She is a clinical therapist and the founder of Mind Potential Publishing, the publishing and marketing specialists to the therapeutic, healthcare and executive coaching industries. She is widely known as the 'Coaches' Coach' and is the creator of the *Control, Program, Rewire (CPR) Brain Training Model* and the *S.C.A.L.E Healthcare Business Model.*

Maggie is the host of the international radio show *'Dare to Shine'* on Law of Attraction Radio Network, Los Angeles and is regularly featured on media worldwide. At the time of writing this, Maggie and Mind Potential Publishing have published over 40 books and online courses, sharing a host of life-changing and inspirational messages with audiences around the globe.

REFERENCES AND RECOMMENDED READING

Download free resources from this book at www.therapistshandbook.com

Institute for the study of therapeutic change
https://scholar.google.com.au/scholar?q=institute+-for+the+study+of+therapeutic+change&hl=en&as_sdt=0&as_vis=1&oi=scholart

Joy Therapy with Dr. Shelley Stockwell
https://scholar.google.com.au/scholar?q=institute+-for+the+study+of+therapeutic+change&hl=en&as_sdt=0&as_vis=1&oi=scholart

International Centre for Clinical Excellence
https://www.centerforclinicalexcellence.com/

Scholarly articles from Scott D Miller
https://scholar.google.com.au/scholar?q=scott+d+miller&hl=en&as_sdt=0&as_vis=1&oi=scholart

Scott D Miller PhD Psychotherapy's missing link – Evolution of Psychotherapy 2017
https://www.youtube.com/watch?v=GHNAv8JnU5E&t=2622s

References and Recommended Reading

The Secrets of Supershrinks: Pathways to Clinical Excellence
www.psychotherapynetworker.org/free-reports

The Outcome of Psychotherapy: Yesterday, Today, and Tomorrow
Psychotherapy 2013 American Psychological Association
2013, Vol. 50, No. 1, 88–97 0033-3204/13/$12.00 DOI: 10.1037/a0031097

A Handbook for Hypnotherapy – Bryan Perry

Creating Connections Volume 1 and 2 – Rob McNeilly

Learning Hypnosis – Rob McNeilly

How to Build a Hypnotherapy Business – Sheila Granger

Stockwell's Hypnosis Dictionary Script Book – Shelley Stockwell-Nicholas

Hypnosis Methods History & Mastery - Shelley Stockwell-Nicholas

UNLEASHED – Maggie Wilde The Potentialist

Unzip the Fat Suit Using Your Mind – Maggie Wilde The Potentialist

MEET THE AUTHORS

Leonie and John O'Connell are joint founders and operate **The Academy of Therapeutic Hypnosis** from the beautiful Blue Mountains in New South Wales, Australia.

They first met almost 40 years ago during their nursing careers and subsequently married and had two children. They have worked together and created successful businesses in childcare and hospitality. Having spent most of their lives working in the caring professions, in 2010, they commenced their journey with hypnotherapy and have never looked back. They now have four grandchildren, run a highly successful hypnotherapy practice in Sydney and provide highly sought-after training courses and mentoring through the Academy.

All graduates through the *Academy of Therapeutic Hypnosis* receive 12-months mentoring and support from Academy instructors after they attend their course. Leonie, John and their other instructors pride themselves on the therapeutic and business support and confidence they instill in their students, many of whom go on to create multiple 6-figure hypnosis clinics.

The Academy of Therapeutic Hypnosis runs courses in all major Australian cities as well as in regional areas, overseas and online.

Please visit our website www.aoth.com.au and see what our graduates have to say or discover the next training dates.

To download free resources from this book go to
www.therapistshandbook.com/resources

WHAT OTHERS HAVE TO SAY

Luke O'Dwyer, Queensland
"Just over a year ago, I was stressed, working long hours, the pay was nothing to write home about… but it was in the area of my lifelong studies, so I thought, "Things will get better if I keep at it. Then I had a health scare which required an operation and some time spent convalescing, and I thought, (rather than feeling sorry for myself), I would use the time more wisely. So I did The Academy of Therapeutic Hypnosis FasTrack course.

Last month, despite the virus epidemic, I clocked double the earnings of my old job, worked much less hours, and instead of being stressed, I take daily inspiration from helping people regain control of their feelings, choices, behaviours and their lives.

Leonie taught me that if you give more than expected, it will come back to you far more than you expected."

Verity Brown, New South Wales
"I trained with The Academy of Therapeutic Hypnosis less than 12-months ago. Within two weeks of completing my training, I had set up my clinic and was confidently working with clients achieving great results.

I very quickly earned more than enough to cover the full cost of my training. Because of Leonie's phenomenal ongoing mentoring and support, I run a successful hypnotherapy practice and with two school-aged boys, I can work my own hours around my family. I love what I do; I am helping people, earning a great income and I know that I am where I am now, only because of Leonie's training and support"

Chris Lucas, New South Wales
"I trained with the Academy of Therapeutic Hypnosis in 2015. I found the course extremely valuable and felt very confident to work with clients immediately.

I have always had back up support, so if I needed help Leonie was always there to assist which boosted my confidence even more. I ended up doing hypnotherapy full-time and I love what I do. My business has grown so much, and it is now supporting our family since my husband had to retire for medical reasons.

I work in a Coffs Harbour and there are 10 hypnotherapists in a very small area, but because of the resources and training I received from **The Academy of Therapeutic Hypnosis***, I am one of the leading hypnotherapists in the area which is something I am very proud of. I highly recommend Leonie's training. The resources and support are amazing."*

Rhys Parry Badkin. Sydney
"I am a life coach and I studied hypnotherapy with the Academy of Therapeutic Hypnosis to add another string to my bow. Having done this course made a huge difference, not only to my skill set but to my cash flow as well, which increased by more than 70%.

The thing about Leonie is that she really cares. The class sizes are small, and learning doesn't stop when the training is over. The ongoing support is phenomenal. Leonie has helped me develop into an increasingly good practitioner and she has really been invested in my success. I would highly, highly recommend training with the Academy."

www.ingramcontent.com/pod-product-compliance
Lightning Source LLC
Chambersburg PA
CBHW070106120526
44588CB00032B/1279